Pr

M000086106

the aging boomers

"*The Aging Boomers* by Frank Samson is an important new contribution to understanding aging and long-term care. It's a must-read for anyone approaching their later years, and for those who have parents about to enter the fourth stage of life. All of the questions that should be asked, and all of the answers you need to hear (from the world's leading experts), are contained in this wonderful new resource. Why wait to experience the challenges of aging when you can learn about it in advance in *The Aging Boomers*?"

DR. S. JAY OLSHANSKY, PH. D.

Professor in the School of Public Health at the University of Illinois at Chicago and author of "The Quest for Immortality: Science at the Frontiers of Aging."

"This book makes it clear that it's what we don't know we don't know that becomes the demise of our good intentions. I am impressed with the depth of insights offered throughout. Readers gain invaluable professional advice that allows them to succeed in the complicated long-term care process."

JOY LOVERDE

Author, "The Complete Eldercare Planner: Where to Start, Questions to Ask, How to Find Help"

"I'm definitely going to recommend *The Aging Boomers* to all my clients, students, and friends. A copy belongs in every household. Straightforward and easy to read, *The Aging Boomers* offers practical tips and resources to do a heartfelt and responsible job of caregiving of our parents as well as highlighting the necessity of maintaining our own life and sanity as we navigate this previously uncharted territory. Frank's expertise, experience, and care shine through every page as he elegantly takes readers through every aspect of this very important topic."

JUDE BIJOU, MA, MFT

Psychotherapist and author of the multi-award winning book, "Attitude Reconstruction: A Blueprint for Building a Better Life."

"Frank Samson, long experienced in the elder care industry, has drawn on a variety of experts he has interviewed, some on his informative radio program, and compiled them into a helpful collection of valuable pieces. He is skilled in drawing out the most important points from those who have contributed to this work. Reading it is like being in a roomful of smart people who can answer all your aging questions."

CAROLYN ROSENBLATT, RN

Elder Law Attorney, Mediator and author of "The Family Guide to Aging Parents: Answers to Your Legal, Financial, and Healthcare Questions."

"Frank's great interviewing skills are at the heart of this book helping to answer the questions we all have when we become caregivers. As he guides real-life caregiver, Linda, through the maze of caregiving, Frank includes advice from experts along the way. I was honored to be included in Frank's book and know readers will find it an insightful, practical, helpful guidebook on their caregiving journey."

SHERRI SNELLING

Author of "A Cast of Caregivers."

"Anyone who has found themselves in the situation of caring and making decisions for an aging loved one needs this book. The extensive assortment of professionals, sharing their knowledge and experience, is a priceless gift to Baby Boomers and people of any age who are having this experience. The book covers a lot of ground — from legal and financial considerations to housing and in-home care to family and emotional considerations —and is organized in a way that enables the reader to pick the sections that will be helpful. Readers will have the benefit of material that will help prepare them for the future, as well. Aside from everything else, this book is a kindness to the many people in search of answers to the myriad questions encountered in aging and caregiving."

MARCY BASKIN, CSA

Eldercare Manager and author of "Assisted Living: Questions I Wish I Had Asked."

the aging boomers

Answers to Critical Questions for You, Your Parents and Loved Ones

Frank M. Samson

DEDICATION

This is for you, Michèle.

Thanks for supporting me all these years.

And for being the best mother and Meme to our wonderful children and grandchildren.

Table of Contents

The Introduction

One fact that cannot be argued is that we're all getting older. Some people will take better care of themselves and will have fewer health challenges as they age. Some just have better genes and may have fewer issues as they age. However, through hundreds of interviews with experts I've had over the past five years, one thing is very clear: many of us are in denial in regard to our potential need for long-term care in the future.

I have had the great opportunity of interviewing some of the most knowledgeable experts on aging, long-term care, and those providing valuable services to seniors. Some of these experts have been highlighted throughout this book, providing a compilation of helpful, practical, and useful advice on the many issues facing boomers, their parents, and our aging population.

I have also had the pleasure of working with families who have a loved one needing assistance — whether the issue is Alzheimer's, Parkinson's Disease, stroke, or just normal aging.

In this book, I will take you on a journey with "Linda," who I will help to navigate through the myriad options and suggestions from our experts.

In this introduction, I want to support you by offering perspectives about your role and by shining a light on some of the specific issues around being a caregiver for elderly parents. The rest of the book goes into further detail, offering resources and expert advice you can lean on as you pull together a plan that works for you and your family.

THE LIKELIHOOD OF NEEDING LONG-TERM CARE

So, what does "long-term care" actually mean? Many think that this term refers to care in a "nursing home" or "convalescent home," terms that are still being used by the public but are long gone in the health care industry. Long-term care refers to needing assistance with your everyday needs, and is sometimes also called "activities of daily living." Examples include assistance with eating, bathing, dressing, toileting, and transferring (walking; moving from place to place).

The challenge is that most people have a misconception as it relates to their own likelihood of needing some type of long-term care. In an interview I conducted with Carol Marak, Senior Care Content Publisher & Marketer for SeniorCare.com, she said, "There is large discrepancy of those who think they will need long-term care versus experts who state that we will need long-term care. The experts say we are in denial."

According to a study highlighted on Senior.com that shows the perception vs. reality of Americans who will need long-term care yields the following results:

- 37% of Americans *think they will* need some sort of long-term care.

- 69% of experts show that *they actually will* need some sort of long-term care.

So, why is there such a drastic difference in people's perception vs. reality? Following are responses from some of the experts that participated in the Senior.com study:

"...human beings have a very limited ability to accurately predict or even really imagine the needs of their future self. This is especially true when that future contains scary possibilities and lies decades in the future."

DR. BILL THOMAS
Wall Street Journal, "Top 10 Americans Shaping Aging"

"Many reasons — but a major one is simple unfamiliarity, which will change in the next few years as Boomers take care of their parents."

DR. JOANNE LYNN
Director, Center for Elder Care and Advanced Illness

"There is not a lack of information about aging issues but there is a lack of knowledge on the part of the consumer about dealing with aging at various stages. Of course, what a person knows about aging depends whether they are the one aging, or if it is a loved one, close relative or someone else farther removed. Often the choice of a care setting is based on the lifestyle of the caregiver, say an employed daughter with a family. Her decisions will be different from someone who can stay at home to provide caregiving services to a loved one, such as a spouse."

TOM BURKE

Senior DirectorAmerican Health Care Association (AHCA)

"While there are many factors, the Foundation's national polling and focus group work shows that most people don't like to think about aging, and particularly the likelihood of growing older with needs. Americans like to think that as we grow older, we will be vibrant and healthy, and then one-day die peacefully in our sleep. As a result, many people choose to not think about, let alone plan for, this time of their life. In addition, many feel that meeting the needs of older loved ones is simply a private family matter. However, seven in ten older Americans will need long-term care at some time in their lives, and 20% will need care for five years or more."

DR. BRUCE CHERNOF

CEO, The SCAN Foundation

"Nobody is actually aging, or at least nobody will admit it. Aging is something that 'only our grandparents do.' Boomers have not accepted that they, too, may need some additional care, like their parents. This is not an aging crisis, but more of a healthcare crisis. Younger populations greatly care and are concerned about the impending needs of their parents, resistance to support, and the high costs associated with it. Our culture as a whole has been driven by acute needs and crisis management versus proactive and preventative care."

LAURA MITCHELL
Consultant on digital health and aging

BOOMERS' ROLE IN AGING

Tina Cheplick has been an RN re-entry program instructor and served on the faculty of UCSF and Cal-State Fullerton. Tina developed care solutions for elders to offer elder care advocacy services, guidance, and training to improve the lives of elders, families, and the individuals who provide care. Her extensive understanding of the aging process, the health care system, and the various medical, legal, and financial issues gives her the ability to create a comprehensive guided care plan that is specific to each elders' and families' needs.

I asked Tina from what she has seen, whether Boomers look at aging differently than maybe generations in the past:

The main thing is that we are starting to reframe aging. Instead of focusing in on limitations, more Boomers are looking at, "What can we do?"

We all know we're not going to escape aging, so that's out there and that's real, but we want to understand more about how we want to live. A big part of that, I think, is making sure that our communities we live in are really helping us to age in place, if you will.

If we look at it statistically, globally we're going to be hitting over 850 million people right now who are over the age of 60. I think that we need to start looking at our communities and helping ourselves, helping the way we live, and how we can maintain a very fulfilling life.

One of the biggest issues we have now, when I consult with Boomers about their parents, is starting the conversation now with our own children about the way we want to live. One of the hottest topics is your power of attorney for health care and the new portable DNR (do not resuscitate), which is the POLST (Physician Orders for Life-Sustaining Treatment).

The topic of elder care often rolls into making sure that families know about their parent's power of attorney for health care, right? The power of attorney for health care usually designates somebody to be the person who would make decisions in the event that the older person could not make decisions for themselves. When we look at the power of attorney for health care, we want to make sure that there's a person in line to do that.

Your power of attorney for health care then rolls into this next step which is the Physician Orders for Life-Sustaining Treatment or the POLST. In other parts of the country, it might be called the MOLST. Basically, it's a form your physician has to fill out and it requires that there be a conversation with the MD that really points out what your options are should you not be able to make decisions for yourself — more like a portable DNR for the elderly.

You can see that it's just an extension of the power of attorney. It reviews the issue of do you want CPR or do you want natural death? Part B is the medical intervention and you get to choose if you want full treatment, elective treatment, comfort-focused treatment? Then Part C is the artificial administration of nutrition. Do you want artificial nutrition through a feeding tube? Then it goes into do you have an advanced directive and then the doctor's signature, and so we know when you go home with this piece of paper and you put it in your house, if the paramedics come, they know exactly what they need to do.

The flip side to it is that the document is very fluid. It can be changed at any time, but it allows people to at least start the discussion about where you want to be should you have an illness and/or you're aging and you have a terminal illness and you want to have some participation in how you want your family to deal with it. I think that's important. When we talk about Boomers, it's really important that we start these discussions as well.

NECESSARY FORMS FOR AGING ADULTS

Though all adults should have a Power of Attorney and DNR (if that is the adult's choice) in place, I wanted Tina to provide more details on the POLST form and on whether this is more for someone who's approaching closer to end-of-life, and with whom the senior should be discussing the details:

Some people want to have it in place in their 70s because maybe they have vascular dementia. I always tell my elders, especially if we're having these very intense conversations, "While you're here and you can participate in the conversation, it's tough, but let's do it. Let's talk about it. Let's get your family and let's talk about what they feel and how they feel about doing it."

I definitely agree, it's important around terminal illness, but I also think it's important to discuss it with those parents. My father had dementia and so I learned first-hand that it was really important to have that discussion with him while he could participate, so when I needed to make the decision, I remembered, and we'd had that conversation that supported me.

SANDWICH GENERATION UNDER PRESSURE

Many people are faced with taking care of a parent, being a parent to children, and working on top of that. I spoke to Sherri Snelling, who is the author of *A Cast of Caregivers* and a nationally recognized expert on America's 65 million family caregivers with her website TheCaregivingClub.com. I asked Sherri to share more about the "Sandwich Generation" and to discuss the challenges they are facing.

The Sandwich Generation is kind of a media buzzword that's out there, and a lot of people may not understand what it means. What it really describes is that collection of caregivers who not only have children who are still at home under the age of 18, or perhaps who've just graduated from college and come back home to stay with mom and dad because it may be hard to find a job out there, but they're also caring for an older parent. It comes from the fact that as a caregiver you're sandwiched between caring for two different generations.

What's really interesting is we often think that this is a typical baby boomer role. We've got aging parents, we're all living longer, and we've got our kids coming back home. Pew Research actually did some research about a year ago and found out that there are more Gen X generation caregivers than baby boomers now. This is not just something that is going to hit us in our 50s and 60s. We have a lot of people who are in their late 30s or their 40s who are now encountering this Sandwich Generation caregiving dilemma.

I often talk about it as the three Cs. You've got children, you've got a career, and now you are caring for a parent. That's a juggling act that's really tough, and the ball that's getting dropped is the ball that says "me." That's why I focus so often on helping caregivers keep that balance, keep all those balls in the air. Don't drop that ball that is talking about self-care.

We know that one out of every two Americans over the age of 85 will develop dementia. That is a huge dilemma for families. It's a real struggle. As we all get older, we've got aging parents who really need our help, and we haven't fully addressed the fact of what are the supports for not only the senior population but also then these caregivers who are struggling to hold down a job.

We know seven out of ten caregivers work, so you've got your responsibilities to your job or your career, your responsibili-

ties to your younger family and spouse, and now you've got your responsibility to your parent. We really need a lot of great resources in place both in the workplace and in communities and through our different state and government agencies to help our society balance this conundrum that we have of just living longer.

HELPING THE CAREGIVER

When I interviewed Sherri, one of the questions I asked her was what caregivers can do when they're caught in that conundrum of being sandwiched between caring for two generations. Her response offers both understanding and practical suggestions:

Focus is really on helping caregivers to understand, "How do I not neglect myself? How do I take care of myself?" Because it's the easiest thing to ignore we give up any kind of exercise. We give up any kind of good nutrition. We're eating on the fly or not eating at all. We're not getting enough sleep. We're dealing with wellness and mental health aspects of maybe the depression over watching an older parent who might be battling an illness like cancer or Alzheimer's. We might have guilt, we're not spending enough time with our kids or our spouse or our friends. All these things are going on, and it really has a lot of negative impact on our own health and wellness.

The bottom line I say to caregivers is if you can't stay healthy then, well, who is going to take care of all these people in your circle? You have to make sure that you're balancing your self-care. Now, easier said than done. I have a program that I write about in my book, and it's on my website and I have some videos. It's called Me Time Monday, and it's kind of a prescription for an easy way to really stay focused on, "Okay, what am I doing for myself?" You take Monday as your start point and you say, "Okay, what am I going to do for myself this week? How am I going to find that time?"

You have a plan for the week. You might have to get some help. You might have to call your sister to watch dad on one of the days you normally would watch him, or you'd have to get a friend to pick up your kids from school because you're just not going to have time because you have to take mom to the doctor's appointment. Whatever it is, get the help so you can find a little bit of time for yourself during the week. That's what Me Time Monday is all about. There's a lot of science behind it, by the way. Johns Hopkins actually did research that Monday is part of our cultural DNA. It's start point for us. It's when we start the workweek, it's when we start the school week, and so it's already kind of ingrained in a start point.

Then, you've got 52 Mondays in the calendar year, so it's not like a New Year's resolution where we make them at the beginning of the year and by June none of us are doing them anymore. We have all these Mondays that we can say, "Gosh, I didn't get my me time in last week, so how am I going to solve it this week?" You have a lot of opportunities to remind yourself to take care of yourself during the week.

MEN TAKING ON CAREGIVING ROLES

We usually think of the daughter of a parent and the mom of the kids, but Sherri provided us with research showing how men now are becoming the key focal point as a family caregiver.

Research is now showing us that men represent 45%, almost half of the family caregivers that are out there, and that's in a primary caregiving role. In the past, we've often seen men be a support to an older parent by maybe helping out with finances or managing some of the legal aspects of caregiving, but now we see men doing a lot of the roles that we would typically think of with women. Again, being the transportation, taking mom or dad to the doctor's office, or helping them modify their home so they can stay living there, getting involved in the physical aspect of caregiving, the feeding, the helping in and out of bed, maybe with a wheelchair.

More and more men are definitely stepping into this role. What's interesting is the Alzheimer's Association, because we mentioned dementia earlier on, found that since 1996, the percentage of men as the primary caregiver of someone with Alzheimer's has doubled. It's gone from 19% in 1996 to 40% just a couple of years ago. That's huge. One of the things I found really interesting, though, is how men and women differ in how they deal with caregiving. There was a great study that came out of Bowling Green State University. It was called Mars Versus Venus. They found that men tend to do a block and tackle approach. They have all these caregiving tasks they have to get done as well as other things in their lives, and they just kind of check it off during the day and move on, whereas women, we are nurturers, but we're also worriers. We overanalyze our caregiving role and responsibilities, and that actually gives women more stress.

While there are more and more men who are caregiving, I want to say just to the ladies, maybe we take a page out of the playbook of the men, because they seem to be actually managing their stress level as caregivers a lot better.

FAMILIES WORKING TOGETHER

Quite often, the burden of making decisions for mom and dad fall on one of the adult children. This can often cause disagreements among siblings. I asked Sherri to shed some light on the roles of siblings and other family members.

I do think you see a lot of that, especially for families who still live close. If grandma and grandpa maybe just live a couple towns over or even in the same city, you're going to find a lot of the children are actually helping out, particularly if they can drive and they can get around. One thing that is a little frightening, and this happens often in more under-served communities, is that we're finding that a lot of these younger children under the age of 18, when a grandparent has moved into the home, the children are stepping up as primary caregivers.

There are actually 1.5 million children under the age of 18 who are primary caregivers. They're feeding and bathing and providing medications to either a grandparent or a parent who might have either certain disabilities or illnesses. The Bill and Melinda Gates Foundation did a wonderful study and it found that, unfortunately, 24% of the kids who are dropping out of high school are dropping out because they are family caregivers. That's a frightening statistic, I think, for all of us. Again, this goes back to how can we help the caregivers? Whether you're 18 years old or 38 years old or 58 years old, let's help caregivers so that they don't have to start sacrificing so many things in their lives.

A ROLE REVERSAL WITH
AGING PARENTS

F. Scott Fitzgerald's 1922 short story, "The Curious Case of Benjamin Button," is a story about a man who starts aging backwards, with bizarre consequences. The movie of the same name that came out in December 2008 was loosely based on Fitzgerald's story. Many who saw the movie, including me, thought that aging backwards is probably the way it should really be.

Well, it's not how it happens, and so if you have aging parents, your children are no longer the only people with whom you take on a parenting role. You're now including taking on the care and decision-making for your own parents. Role reversal for aging parents is difficult for all concerned.

This is the day you thought would never happen. Your roles in life are reversing. You are trying to make decisions for yourself and your aging parent. What will be best for them without altering your life too drastically? How do you keep up the pace and ultimately please everyone around you? You are not alone in life; you have a family, significant other, and a career to think about. You want to balance everything, to keep everyone happy and for life to remain as normal as possible. Think again! Those once a week visits or daily phone calls may not be enough anymore. Your parent needs care, the real kind.

Care includes making sure they eat, that they take their meds, that their money isn't being squandered away on TV shopping. You have siblings who think assisted living or nursing facilities are awful and they don't want to put mom or dad in one, even though they also don't want to help out. How do you cope? How do you deal with this situation without alienating every member of your family?

This is not about guilt or what some think is of as the "right" thing to do. It is not about hanging on to someone to stay how they used to be. An elderly person in your care may be in need of constant care and attention. If you need a dose of growing up, this situation will make it happen, whether you're ready or not!

SON OR DAUGHTER AS CAREGIVER

How do you begin to manage all the issues regarding caring for your elderly parents? Start with their doctor. Make an appointment to discuss the health of your beloved parent. Between the doctor and senior care advisors, you may be able to determine the types of help and living style your parent's current status requires. Keep asking questions until you have determined the best situation for all concerned.

It may not be as simple as a caregiver visiting a few times a week to help with showering, dressing, meals, and meds. Their health needs may require more than that and asking the visiting nurse or doctor's office is the place to go to with your concern.

The best word to learn to help an elder parent is the same as if your infant child was being cared for, and that is *safety*. If safety is not at the level necessary, keep pushing until you get the help you need. Keep insisting on safety.

It may take you time to uncover everything available to your parent to help with their care process but trust me, it will be worth it in the many years elder care can stretch out to be. It is best to discuss with them all their health and medical, financial, and personal situations before that day arrives when care is needed.

When your parent is older, the best thing you can give them is you. Spend quality time instead of stress time. Have them over for a day and dinner instead of pawning them off on someone else. The resentment builds if you do this alone. There are many really good options out there to take that burden off your shoulders.

LONG-DISTANCE CAREGIVING

Today, children who live far from their loved ones can monitor a parent's health using their computers or phones and medical devices inside the senior's home.

Long-distance caregiving continues to be a growing trend, with difficult challenges for adult children. The Pew Research Center estimates that one out of every eight adults in America between the ages of 40 and 60 is raising children of their own and tending to aging parents. Plus, between seven and ten million adults care for their parents from far away.

Every aspect of caregiving tends to be difficult from afar, including determining the level of care needed, finding good local care providers, and managing the quality of care. The greatest challenges for long-distance caregivers include how to know when a senior needs help, given that their loved one sounds perfectly fine on the phone and perhaps in emails or letters. Other difficulties include not knowing how to aid local siblings with caregiving, finding local professional caregiving help, checking up on a parent's medical care, and finding time to visit them to help take care of their personal affairs, financial paperwork, and residential safety.

Other challenges include providing respite care for a live-in caregiver, helping parents decide if it may be time to move from their residence to a safer environment, like assisted living, and not being present for the whole period of time when a parent's life may be ending.

Many long-distance caregivers feel guilty about not doing enough and concern themselves with having the ability to afford taking time away from work, leaving their family, and all the costs associated with travel.

A good way to meet these challenges is to generate a solid care plan for the senior. *The Family Caregiver Alliance Handbook for Long-Distance Caregivers* has a step-by-step guide for families to help them:

- Assess the care status

- Develop a care team

- Hold a family meeting

- Access local agencies

Determine exactly what the senior needs help doing and how much assistance is necessary. Is help needed with activities of daily living (ADLs), including dressing, bathing, eating, transferring oneself, and toileting? What about cooking, shopping, household tasks, laundry, and taking medications? Observe the senior during the day and find out which activities are the most challenging. Ask the senior where support is needed most. Chatting with the senior's doctor can also help determine where help would be beneficial. A detailed understanding saves time and expense in the end, because the help received is well aligned with the senior's needs.

The adult child needs to be sure they've gotten written permission to receive their parent's medical and financial information. Onsite caregivers should be aware of exactly what the family wants should the senior becomes ill or has an accident.

Family meetings, along with other communications, have become easier to coordinate through web conference calls, video chatting, texting, and personal websites. Regular conference calls are a way to get updated on a parent's health.

Today, children who live far from their loved ones can monitor a parent's health using their computers or phones by installing medical devices inside the senior's home that measure and distribute vital signs, oxygen saturation, blood-sugar readings, weight, temperature, and motion detection. The Internet communicates the results to the senior's family and doctor.

Overseeing the care of loved ones from afar increases emotional and psychological stress. Many community and online resources, support groups, and organizations offer help and guidance. Though each person's situation is unique, with the right support from others, as well as the senior's involvement wherever possible, the adult child living a long way away will feel more at ease knowing their aging parent is safe and taken care of.

DON'T LET GUILT GET IN
THE WAY OF PROPER CARE

The number one fear of older adults is losing their independence and, often, adult children trigger that fear when they tell their aging parents what to do.

I give advice to adult children every day about their parents or other family members. Though many issues are discussed, first and foremost, safety is the number one priority. When the safety of someone you love and care about is in question, it can lead to strong emotions and stress.

Many feel an enormous weight of guilt and sometimes even a sense of failure for the inability to care for aging parents. Guilt, helplessness, and the pain of realizing that you may no longer be suited or able to give your elderly parent what he or she needs is a huge burden for any child to feel (regardless of age), and it will take time and a lot of patience to be able to deal with such feelings a parent's care.

Coming to a decision that your parent may need more specialized care and time than you are able to personally provide is not easy. When assessing the need for more specialized elderly care for your parent, you may need to take the following issues under consideration:

- Is my parent able to stay safe in the current living environment?

- Can I devote the time necessary to adequately care for my elderly parent's needs?

- Do I have it in me to handle my parent suffering from a cognitive disorder such as Alzheimer's?

- Am I able to help my aging parent with mobility issues?

However, any such decision often brings with it a heavy toll such as feeling like:

- Should I be doing more? Should I be doing it better?

- Am I doing things right?

- Is my elderly parent too much of a burden for me?

- I'm so tired!

- I just want my old life back!

- I'm inadequate, ill equipped, and emotionally weak.

When feeling guilty, adult children often tell parents what to do and they do this with the best of intentions. The number one fear of older adults is losing their independence and, often, adult children trigger that fear when they tell their aging parents what to do. Aging parents then become less willing to share information about their health or struggle to continue to live independently. The result is typically some sort of accident or crisis, exactly the outcome the adult child was hoping to prevent. The senior gives in to their kids' demands and just try to get by. They may become unhappy, depressed, and withdrawn.

A different approach is to share your concerns with your parents. Use "I" language as much as possible, since the word "you" tends to make others defensive and stop listening. For example, instead of saying, "You should move, since you can't be alone anymore," you may want to say, "It's becoming very difficult on me and the rest of the family to travel so many hours to see you." Ask your parents for their ideas on how to solve the problem. This step is a process and will not be solved with just one conversation.

In a book by William Bakkus called *Telling Yourself the Truth*, he brings up the following points to caregivers who feel guilty:

1. You did not cause this disease.

2. Your loved one would not have wanted you to stop living.

3. Being a caregiver was one of the most noble and wonderful things anyone can do for a loved one.

4. You did the best you could under the most extreme care-giving circumstances.

Be willing to compromise. Is it more important that your parents make some changes or that nothing changes? Listening and respecting your parent's opinions can also increase the chances they'll be willing to make further changes in the future.

It is important that you give yourself some time to adjust or to let all of those feelings out or to grieve. Just know that the goal is to begin living again while keeping your loved one safe.

CHAOTIC TO CALM CAREGIVING

Pamela Spahr is a leading expert in behavioral techniques designed especially for caregivers to effectively manage patients with dementia and Alzheimer's Disease. She's also a nationally recognized speaker, conducting work-shops and advanced training for caregivers.

Several years ago Pamela's husband suffered several strokes and, as a result, he was diagnosed with dementia. When he came home from the hospital he didn't come with an instruction guide. It took her months to figure out how to manage her husband on a daily basis because his behaviors were entirely different than before he had the dementia.

After several months of trying to figure out how to work with him, she remembered that years before, she had learned how to effectively communicate with people using certain behavioral techniques which turned out to be a lifesaver for her. I asked that she share this information for other caregivers out there who may have the same problems where these techniques could apply.

One of the things that caregivers, especially new caregivers, have to understand is that people with dementia and Alzheimer's are very, very susceptible to the state of their caregiver's behavior or mind. If a person approaches a loved one who has dementia, and that person or caregiver is agitated, it will only make the patient more agitated.

One of the first things I teach is a technique called "low, slow, and in the flow." It just means you approach somebody slowly. You talk softly and slowly. You try to get them to move at your pace, which is now very calm. By showing them that calmness you give them permission to be calm.

One of the other techniques I use is to observe your loved one. I don't mean looking at how they physically look. What I mean is, are they moving slowly? If they're moving slowly, they may be calm. Are they moving fast? They may be agitated. If a loved one is agitated, using different techniques to calm them down is required. If they're calm and the caregiver is calm, then both of them will be working in unison together. It's a much better state to be in to elicit cooperation.

IMPORTANCE OF TONE IN YOUR VOICE

So many people compare the similarities of taking care of an adult to taking care of a child. However, raising your voice or talking to an adult like a child is certainly not going to help the situation. I asked Pamela to comment on that, as well as on how she deals with taking her husband out publicly.

When I brought my husband home, I thought I would use my everyday tone. I was a high-tech executive, so I tended to put a lot of authority in my voice. I had every day planned. I knew when he was going to get up and when he was going to go to bed, and what we were going to do during the day. Then I would talk to him in this very authoritative voice. One day he looked right at me and he said, "Pam, don't talk to me that way. I'm not a child." I learned in a hurry that I had to change my whole strategy and that authoritative voice wasn't going to fly.

I'm a very forgiving caregiver. I take my husband everywhere. I take him out to dinner every once in a while. I take him out to breakfast. I take him to events. I take him to some business events. I have a very helpful technique that I use when I take him out. I have a little business card that says on it, "The person with me has dementia. Your patience is appreciated." I will give that to a server, or a clerk, or if a person approaches him, I'll give it to them. It maintains respect for my husband but it also lets other people know that he had dementia and he may say odd things. He may ask some odd questions. He may touch someone when they don't expect it, maybe on the arm or on the shoulder or something. Now they feel much more comfortable that they know what the situation is.

MANAGING STRESS WITH A BODY-CENTERED APPROACH

One of the great challenges during the aging process, especially as a caregiver for a loved one, is dealing with the stress of the particular situation and everything surrounding this situation. Self-awareness is a key factor for lowering stress and boosting peak performance. I have had the pleasure of interviewing Steve Sisgold on more than one occasion. Steve is an author, speaker, trainer, and executive coach who has spent 25 years studying and teaching about the relationship between beliefs held in the body and success. Steve suggests using body-centered approaches rather than mental approaches for reducing stress. I asked him to explain the difference between those two approaches and the effectiveness of each:

Like Einstein said, "You can't solve a problem with the same thinking that created it." A lot of our stress comes from thinking about stuff that happened; that we wish would have happened differently, so we have a lot of regrets. We also think about the future, of course. Very little time is spent in the actual moment, thinking, "Hmm, what's happening for me right now?" We approach stress from a mental stance. We think or say, "Well, maybe I can think differently," or "Maybe I'll just hold it in and not tell anybody," or "It will just go away."

But what it does is put us up into our nervous system. We have two pieces to the nervous system. There's the sympathetic, which is that fight or flight up in our chest, and then there's the more relaxed in our belly, parasympathetic.

When we're in that sympathetic, our digestive system shuts down. Our heart beats fast. Our blood pressure goes up, so we can climb that tree if a tiger is chasing us. But, unfortunately, with all the modern stress, the machines, the screens, the new information coming at us so much, a lot of us don't realize that that stress is building, and we're basically living in that fight or flight most of the time. The body can only take so much, and the stress will show up in disease, or show up in somebody that's normally kind, all of a sudden being hauled off to jail for hitting somebody. That's the rage that builds within us.

The stats are pretty well known: 80% to 90% of doctor's visits are stress-related. I think it's time for us to really take a look at things we can't change or control outside of us, necessarily. What we can change is the reaction we have to things, which is what stresses us out. It's how we react to things.

A body-centered approach to stress involves paying attention to what's happening in your body at any given moment. Just start with noticing how your body feels. The benefits received from what our bodies tell us is dependent upon how well we listen to our own body and how we respond.

INFORMATION OVERLOAD VERSUS LONGEVITY

I asked Steve to comment on the relationship between information overload and stress. The fact that people are bumping into poles on the street as they're typing a text in their phone is pretty sad. Steve's comments were very insightful to this issue:

First of all, I think we don't even realize that no matter who you are, you're looking down at that phone. Just think about that. Your neck is bent down, and now they're finding we have more neck, vertebrae, back muscles, shoulder tension than ever before. That's because we're staring down all the time. Four hours, three hours, an hour at a time, not even realizing it.

Also, the number one reason for longevity, and it's been studied throughout the world, is community. Many are sitting there staring at our phones, families sitting around a table and everybody's on their machines. More people live alone today, and they never lived alone before. The elders always had their grandchildren and their family. They all woke up together. The elders were very busy, whether it was picking food, or cooking, or helping with the kids. Now there's isolation.

The second thing that they found is movement. A lot of us, because we're sitting with screens and TVs, and I'm just shocked sometimes when I talk to people. I know, because I have to make myself move just like everybody else, but then it becomes a habit. I get up in the morning. I move, I breathe, I go swim. I make that the priority. I take my dog for a walk. Whatever it is. If you start the day with movement and community, you're going to have less stress. It's going to set a tone for your day.

If you're starting your day with these machines and this virtual world, number one, you're hurting yourself physically because your posture usually isn't good if you're staring at a machine or screen. If you'll notice, you're probably crunched over. Then secondly, it's keeping us from real sense of community, as I said.

Not just getting exercise, but getting up and moving more than sitting makes a huge difference in how much stress piles up in our bodies. It's kind of sad. I've talked to people that were rushing to that publisher meeting in New York City, and didn't realize because they were looking at their phone, and stepped off the curb and they're limping into the publisher's meeting. That's not a joke. It's for real. I hear about it all the time.

As you focus on caring for your parents in a way that also works for you, keep in mind that you will find strength by minimizing your information overload, building and relying on community for support, and taking time for yourself by moving each day.

BLUE ZONES

There are areas around the world referred to as Blue Zones — places where longevity is higher than average. There is proof that people live significantly longer in some parts of the world than in others. Steve Sisgold provided his perception of this phenomenon and what can we learn from it.

Some explorers went around looking for people that were living over 100, living peaceful, living healthy. They went around and they watched and circled on the map these areas with a blue marker. They called them Blue Zones.

I was in a place called Yelapa, Mexico. They didn't have electricity. I didn't know it was called a Blue Zone back then, but I guess I experienced it. Number one was community. No one felt isolated. No one felt useless. Everyone had a purpose, whether you were watching the baby, whether you were boiling water, whether you were sweeping the front porch. Everybody got up. No one woke up depressed with nothing to do. That's number one — community purpose.

Secondly, everyone moved most of the time. There was very little sitting until nighttime. Basically during the day, no matter what your age was, you got up, you did something. You did some sort of movement. Like I said, from sweeping, to cooking, to walking with the kids, going to the store. Whatever it was. Then, at night, the sun would go down and there would be a whole community of people, together — singing, talking, telling funny stories, going to bed when it got dark, waking up with the light.

Then the third thing they found is that they ate very simply. They ate mostly a plant diet. Lots of fruits, lots of vegetables, lots of fiber, and of course they grew it and it was fresh. These are people I saw, and it's really interesting, because besides being a Blue Zone, when I talked to these people, –I was there asked to do some work with the group — and people were making noise. Releasing stress, releasing trauma, different things that they carried in their bodies. When I talked to some of the leaders of the community, this non-electric, indigenous kind of community, they didn't know a couple of things. They said, "We don't know what you mean by 'they're carrying stuff in their past, or thinking about the future.'" They had no idea what that concept meant. They're not worried about the future. They're not thinking about anything that happened yesterday.

I guess the main thing I want to say is to take control now. Do something that you can do to take control of your life. If you're not exercising and you can, get up and start walking, breathing properly, eating better, communicating better, and trying to connect with people. Get social. I tell people, go to a bookstore signing, or go to a talk.

Those people in Yelapa woke up with the sun. They didn't wake up and watch TV or turn on the radio or go to their laptop. What do you do? You wake up and you get out in your community. Everybody's up with the roosters, and you're working.

I've been to certain cultures. I've traveled a lot on this subject, and I never see people sitting around. They just wake up and boom. Somebody's outside sweeping. Somebody's getting water. Somebody's cooking. The kids are picking vegetables. We used to be very physical. We used to be more internal, meaning we felt our bodies. We felt our sweat. We felt the sun on our body. Now we're more external. We're looking at screens. We're talking on phones. We're looking at TV. We're watching other people's lives through these reality shows.

REBOOTING TECHNIQUE

Steve has coined a phrase he calls his "rebooting technique" which is just another way of saying to unplug. That may be easier to say and hard to do, so I asked Steve how people could accomplish this when they are confronted with so many issues in their lives:

I guarantee you if your computer or your TV goes down, and you call for help, you'll probably reach somebody in India or some foreign country, and they're instructed to tell you to reboot. They're going to tell you to turn it off and recharge it. Unfortunately, we don't do that very often for ourselves. Right now, I'm working with groups and patients, and also even corporations where I'm having people twice a day reboot, meaning you unplug. You shut down everything. If it's five minutes twice a day, you just take a chance to shut everything down. Let the brain relax, because the brain is overworked.

When you're multitasking and talking to someone, you're using one part of your brain. If you're e-mailing, you're using a different part of your brain... shooting sparks back from one part of the brain to the other until it gets drained, exhausted, or you press send, and are sorry you sent it. It's just too much of the mental and external.

It's an unplug, and then focus on your breath. Just notice it. Are you breathing in your chest or your belly? Even now.

Just notice. You'll learn about yourself. Take notice. Are you shaking your legs? Are you crunched up? Is your fist tight? Is your belly? Are you breathing in your chest? Again, become aware and scan your body. If you're all crunched up right now, uncrunch. If you're bent over, sit up straight. Just notice. Be aware of your body experience.

People should just breathe and relax and visualize the ocean or a brainwave. It will usually calm the brain down. For most of us, our brain is working way too much, too stimulated. Just kind of right now, if you want to focus on a brainwave, or an ocean wave, just see it coming in on the in breath, just send it out on the out breath. Notice how your body starts to relax, and you get in touch with, how you can let go of that stress on every out breath.

Then people need to decide what they're going to do next, meaning my action is, "I'm going to cook", or "I'm going to do something". Get focused. It really helps. When we're scattered, it just keeps the brain scattered. It's pretty much breathing, scanning the body, making adjustments so your body can be more relaxed, seeing a wave for a few breaths and relaxing your brain, and then picking one thing to do, instead of ten. Do this twice a day.

When this was tested at the doctor's office with machines, there was a 55% reduction in stress, and erratic heartbeats went to coherent heartbeats. Basically, breathing, scanning,

relaxing the body is going to get you in a much healthier
state, more relaxed, but also really good for the heart, and
the lungs, and blood pressure.

STORY OF LINDA

The previous sections of this Introduction chapter provide an overview of some of the important issues facing long-term caregivers and relatives. In subsequent chapters, I am going to help counsel a woman named Linda through figuring out how to care for her elderly parents. I'll share my experience and bring in experts on various issues to further support Linda on her journey. I'm going to help Linda reduce the stress of her situation.

Everybody's story is different in so many ways, but the process of dealing with the issues facing parents, spouses, and other loved ones are very comparable.

Let me tell you about Linda. She may be a lot like you.

Linda is in her early 50s and part of the Sandwich Generation, where she is literally sandwiched between aging parents who need care while helping and support-ing her own children. She works full-time in the local school district, is married and has three children, two in their early 20s and one teenager who needs special medical attention. She has two siblings, a sister who lives on the other side of the country, and a brother who resides in Mexico.

Linda worries about her parents, which keeps her up at night. Linda's mother, 84, has vascular dementia and her father, 86, has early stage dementia, though not officially diagnosed. Her parents live together in a small mobile home park and are not safe living there alone. Her father has rejected any caregivers coming to assist them, does not want to move, and said that he can take care of his wife just fine. Neighbors have expressed safety concerns about Linda's parents to the management of the Mobile Home Park.

Linda has been talking to co-workers who have convinced her that she needs to move her mother or both of them to a safer environment where there is 24-hour care. However, her parents do not have much money put away, and due to their daughter's medical condition and other college tuitions, Linda and her husband do not have the funds to provide the additional financial support they need.

TAKING THE NECESSARY STEPS

Throughout this book, I will counsel Linda on various topics, to educate and empower her and to help her take the steps that are right for her, her parents, and her family. The topics we'll look at include:

- Best ways of communicating with her parents and other family members

- Getting proper legal and medical advice

- Options to consider when having to pay for long-term care

- What to know when considering home care, assisted living or nursing

- Elder care scams and abuse and what to watch for

- Ensuring she takes care of herself as a caregiver

The primary way I help people with this sometimes difficult process is to make sure they are getting the best answers to their questions, meaning the answers that inform them according to their own situation and that provide them with relief and viable solutions.

As Linda asks questions and focuses on finding the best answers, she figures out how to make the best decisions for herself and her family.

CHAPTER ONE

Family Communications

Most people want to live independently as long as possible, but many of the Baby Boomers are dealing with a parent or loved one who needs care at some level. This can range from everyday tasks such as meal preparation, assistance with errands, driving to doctors or activities. The need may also arise for assistance to move into a retirement or independent living community, assisted-living community or even a nursing home. It is essential to communicate with an elderly parent or loved one about the possibility of the various care options should the need arise.

The term "aging in place" is a term being used in the senior care industry for helping someone live at home instead of considering other options. Of course, most seniors want to stay at their own home, but the family must consider safety as the number one priority.

Linda's parents are no different. Her mother, who has mid-stage dementia, is willing to do whatever Linda's father is willing to do. Her father, who also is having some cognitive and physical issues, wants to stay home and says he can take care of his wife. However, I did pose the following questions to Linda regarding her parents:

- Have there been medication mistakes?

- Has wandering away from home occurred?

- Is there weight loss due to lack of food and/or fluid?

- Have there been falls?

- Has the stove or toaster oven been left on?

- Is there a need for nighttime supervision?

- Is there a need for daytime supervision if alone for an extended period of time?

With the exception of the wandering issue, the answers to all the above questions were "yes," without hesitation. Linda's relationship with her mother was much stronger through the years than her father. However it was time for her family to have a discussion among themselves.

I contacted some experts in the field in regards to Linda's situation so she and her siblings take the right approach with her parents.

FAMILY PLANNING FOR ELDER CARE

Joy Loverde is recognized as one of the leading experts on successful aging and eldercare. She works with family members and organizations that want to lessen the financial and emotional burdens of caring for elderly loved ones.

One thing that I discussed with Joy in regard to Linda's situation is the fact that her family should have planned, but they did not. That's the reality of it. They waited for something to happen that would require action rather than anticipating and being proactive. Linda's mom and dad had falls and her mom has some things going on cognitively, but now it's getting more serious. I asked Joy how she advises families to plan:

Well, I lead by example. I advise families to plan, and then tell everyone else. This is the theory of "I'll go first." If I take a look at what must be done, let's say from a legal point of view, that means maybe putting a will together, putting together finances and having a power of attorney for healthcare. You need to get your own act together first, and then go around to the family say, "Here's what you need to know about my plan for the future." What I do is I get my stuff done first, and then I give it and distribute it as is at should be, to everyone else around me, including aging parents. Then I say, "Okay, I'm done. Now it's your turn." We can't expect other people to do this kind of planning if we haven't done it ourselves, right? Set an example and then insist on having them at least begin the process. Have them start somewhere. Maybe the easiest place to start is the power of attorney for healthcare.

POWER OF ATTORNEY

Linda's parents do not have a power of attorney document in place. I wish the name of this document was different, because when people hear "Power of Attorney," they think, "I have to go to my attorney. It's going to get expensive. I don't want to deal with it now." Even though it's called power of attorney, it's not necessary to use an attorney to complete this form, though it's always good to have an attorney help you. Joy agreed with me and added this advice:

In fact, that form is free. You can get it anywhere. You can get it at a hospital. You can get it at the local department on aging. You could get it at a nursing home. You could download it on the Internet and, as long as it's designated by the state where you live, you're good to go.

Linda needs to understand that when dealing with parents in their 80s or even 90s, when they sign a power of attorney form, they're not signing over their independence or their decision making. They form will become helpful if they're get into a situation where they are not able to make the decisions, but as long as they're able to make decisions, even though they've signed a power of attorney, they're fine with continuing to do that.

Having a power of attorney form is especially helpful in the event of needing to sell real estate owned by the aging parents. For instance, if you need to sell their house because you have to pay for long-term care for your parents, and if your parents are both owners of the house, the children will need the power of attorney form. Maybe the parent already has a power of attorney form that designates each other. Either way, should one or the other of the parents become incapacitated, you can't sell someone else's house without having power of attorney. That's a great reason to get going on getting one in place right now.

I was in a situation where we couldn't sell real estate because one of the people became incapacitated They had claimed that they had power of attorney, but my mistake was not actually seeing the document ahead of time. We had assumed it was in the box in the closet. You know, the famous box in the closet where all the papers are kept? Or the file. When I had asked, "You have power of attorney?" Though the answer was "Yes," the reality turned out to be no.

In Linda's situation, she and her brother went to her parents and tried to explain power of attorney to them. They're in a situation where they're starting to have cognitive issues, and they said, "No. We don't need to do that. I'm okay, I can make my own decisions." Now what? Joy had some input:

Well, no does not necessarily mean no in elder care land. It means, 'I heard you, and I don't have to answer this right now. No doesn't mean no. It's just a time saver sometimes for people who are afraid to face what needs to be done. Perhaps we're not the right person to bring up that very sensitive subject, or perhaps we can invite someone else to bring it up, like an attorney, or a doctor, or sometimes it's a daughter or son in law, someone who has less of an edge in these very sensitive conversations. Consider the fact that we may not be the best person for the job if it's a matter of bringing up a touchy subject with our own parents.

FINANCIAL CONSIDERATIONS

Many adult children, like Linda and her siblings, don't want to put the financial stress on their own children that they may be going through with their parents. I usually hear, "Well, that's just too expensive." Joy gave me her thoughts about putting long-term care insurance in place as a way to relieve this worry.

I don't see long-term care insurance as something that's purchased only to address the issue of aging. It is definitely available to anyone over the age of 18 years old. Anything can happen to us at any time that may require us to have long-term care in an institutional setting, or at home. I look at it as part of a healthy financial portfolio. The earlier we procure the policy, the better. And then at some point if it looks like later on your finances are fine, and you've maintained a healthy lifestyle, and it doesn't look like you're going to need it, when you get to be in the upper ages, you can drop it. Then you're done, but it's still in place and it really is a safety net.

I have a good friend who has Parkinson's. He's been in assisted living over twelve years. He literally could not survive the lifestyle that he has without long-term care insurance.

Insurance companies sell a combination life and long-term care, which is a great combination because as you get older, and the kids are off on their own, and they're doing okay, maybe you don't need as much life insurance, but you're going to need more long-term care.

The other thing is if you wait too long, you won't qualify for long-term care insurance. If you wait too long, your health may not allow you to even qualify, so why not purchase it when you're healthy?

KEEPING RELATIONSHIPS INTACT

I told Joy that Linda doesn't have the best relationship with her father, and that telling her father, "You need more help. You need to move" didn't go over very well.

Well, as it relates to the planning part, keep in mind the successful stories that I hear from caregivers are the ones who have kept the relationship intact. Sometimes when we're on a path to solve a problem with loved ones, as it relates to planning ahead, if we treat the people we're talking to like they're a problem to solve, we're going to get in some hot water with the relationship. Once the relationship is damaged, we're going to be hard pressed to get it back on track.

The stories that I love to listen to from caregivers are the ones where they say, "We have this incredible relationship, and a respectful relationship, and we did this planning under those circumstances." That means that a lot of people, caregivers, were patient and they were kind, and not in a hurry to treat their parents and loved ones like they were a problem. That stance produces the best outcomes.

Linda can't forget the relationship. Everyone is in the same boat. They're all doing this together. If she can, have her ask questions rather than make statements. It might take a little longer, but in the long run, if you keep that relationship intact, everyone will be better off.

I'm in this situation right now with an elderly aunt. It's very clear to me that she is having difficulty at home, however, she sees it quite differently. She is in love with staying home, and will do anything, even if safety is an issue, to stay there. I have been working with her for over three years on the idea about moving. You can imagine my patience level has to be very, very high, especially when I see her getting in trouble in terms of safety.

Now she continues to tell me she is not moving, no matter what. I continue to raise the trust level with her not by telling her she has to move, but by being prepared myself for anything to happen. When things happen, I'm there. We take care of the problem, and she stays put. The other thing is that from time-to-time she is more willing to accept people coming in to help her when she needs it. There will come a time, unfortunately, in this situation, where something may happen, and she will be out of options and choices on where she goes next. My aunt and I have had this frank conversation, and she understands that this is the consequence she may be paying by staying at home, but out of respect for her and my relationship with her, this is the way it's going to be.

A lot of elderly people would say, "Okay, well I'm ready to go. Let's go." Maybe someday my aunt will call me and say, "I'm ready." That's what my mom did. But, again, with my mom, it took me five years of being there for her.

UNDERSTANDING DEMENTIA AND FAMILY CHALLENGES

Laurie White works with families who have a relative with dementia and is a memory care program consultant for assisted living companies. Laurie is also a noted presenter at educational conferences for both professional and family caregivers. Laurie is very well respected in the field of dementia and family communications relative to this subject.

I asked Laurie to help educate Linda on dementia since Linda's mother has been diagnosed with what they believe is vascular dementia. Her father, though not diagnosed at this time, is having short-term memory and other cognitive issues. I felt it was important for Linda to have a good understanding of dementia and the various types of dementia. Laurie provided this insight:

When I entered the field of dementia 30 years ago, we were just learning to talk about Alzheimer's disease. We were having problems even pronouncing it. Some people, I remember, back then called it "Oldzheimer's Disease" because back in the early 80s, we were still calling people who had symptoms of confusion and disorientation and some behavioral changes "senile." Thankfully, we moved away from that term because we recognize that not all people who get old become confused or disoriented. Then we began to recognize Alzheimer's as a specific disease.

The 1990s were dedicated as the decade of the brain. Indeed, we learned a lot about Alzheimer's in those ten years. We increased our research about the brain, but we still have a long way to go. I would say that we have a greater understanding of Alzheimer's and dementia, but the confusing part for many people is that we use the terms Alzheimer's Disease and dementia interchangeably. It gets to be very confusing. Let me just take a moment to see if I can shed some light on that.

"Dementia" is a term that we use to describe a group of symptoms: memory loss, language difficulties, problems with spatial and depth perception, attention span problems, maybe even personality and mood changes. You can have some of those symptoms and changes for a variety of reasons. The next question is then what type of dementia might it be. Because Alzheimer's Disease is the most common form of dementia, accounting for about 50 to 75 percent of the types of dementia, it's understandable why we use those terms interchangeably. The bottom line is that Alzheimer's Disease is the most common form of dementia. It is only one form of dementia.

Other forms of dementia include Lewy Body Dementia, which is gaining a lot of attention recently and some people say is the second leading cause of dementia. That's a little bit different than Alzheimer's disease but just share some of the symptoms. Most likely not in the same order and has more physical symptoms with it than Alzheimer's does in the beginning stages.

Then, of course, there is vascular dementia, which is commonly stroke related. There are a lot of other forms of dementia, but one that also is, I would say, on the horizon in the last maybe five to ten years is mixed dementias. Basically what that means is you could have not one type of dementia but you could have two or more types of dementia. You can have Alzheimer's Disease and vascular dementia. Both of those types of dementia will affect the brain, which then account for changes in behavior and perhaps changes in mood and personalities, but will affect overall abilities, for sure.

Since Linda's mom has been diagnosed with vascular dementia and her dad is starting to show signs of cognitive impairment, if she gains some perspective and learns about her parents' specific forms of dementia, it will help Linda more effectively make decisions about their care.

SIBLING ISSUES

Both of Linda's siblings live out of town, her sister on the opposite coast and her brother in Mexico. Both of them are in some sort of denial relative to their parent's situation; especially her brother, who only sees his parents once a year. Linda is having challenges explaining the reality of the situation to them. Laurie offers these suggestions:

Many people are just very fearful about aging parents. I think it's very difficult to accept something that we don't easily see, like the effects of dementia, especially if we're not spending a lot of time with the elderly person. We see some changes and abilities and perhaps even some changes in behavior. Because they can change every day, we don't really understand what's going on or why they are changing, why a person's abilities are changing every day. I think with the increasing numbers of people who are in their 60s and 70s, Baby Boomers, is that people are fearful of getting dementia. It's like if we don't talk about it, it doesn't exist. But this is too big a problem to ignore.

What we know is that acceptance of the symptoms then leads to, in many cases, acceptance of the diagnosis. What we know from some of the research that's been done is that it can take two, two and a half years, for family members to understand that their relative's changing abilities have been increasing over the last couple of years. Family members can be confused about whether these changes just due to dad getting older or is it something more serious? Oftentimes, there are a couple of years delay in getting that diagnosis.

Then there is the issue of accepting it and grieving, because that diagnosis of dementia has a pretty big impact. I'm thinking about a husband that I met with the other day who was really having a difficult time dealing with his wife's Alzheimer's disease. He kept saying, "Well, she won't do this and she won't wash her hair and she ..." It's really repetitive and he was going on to describe someone who was probably entering the middle stages. He stopped in his tracks and he said, "I guess I need to change my expectation of her, don't I?"

It's acceptance of the diagnosis as well as acceptance and recognition of the symptoms that care partners also have to change, to change the way they view their relative and to see them in a different light. Because their relative is changing, the way they talk to their relative has to change. As all these changes are taking place, at the same time family members are taking on more responsibility. I think acceptance of the diagnosis, understanding what the diagnosis means is sometimes quite a task.

I also think after acceptance there's an adjustment that's needed in attitude. How is this diagnosis, whether it's Alzheimer's disease or vascular dementia, how is that affecting the care partner's attitude? What I hear a lot from care partners is they're very sad. In fact, they're grieving because they are observing their relative and that relative can't do what he or she can't do.

Then the other thing, of course, and this is a really hard thing for many families to do, is to recognize that the rel-

ative really is trying as hard as they can. Sometimes when you're a care partner, like Linda's father is for her mother, you get so frustrated and so tired that it's really hard to have that recognition. You are trying very hard and your relative who has dementia is also trying very hard. When it seems like maybe if they just try harder, they could do better, which often is not the case at all that they are putting all their effort into staying involved, trying to maintain a "normal life" as the disease progresses.

Also, how to manage what's to come but also staying focused on the present, whether that is today and tomorrow or months ahead, whatever that may be, but not to get too far ahead of themself; if we look, what I found through the years is that caregivers often want a lot of answers about what's to come. As you know, we can't give them a definitive schedule of when the changes are going to take place because everyone is so very different.

As Laurie mentioned repeatedly, acceptance by the family members as to the symptoms and to the diagnosis is key to getting her siblings support. I think Linda's siblings need to visit and see for themselves, because it all starts with acceptance.

BEHAVIOR ISSUES

Linda brought up to Laurie some of her issues and talked about the behaviors happening with her father. He is becoming very short with her, which he never was in the past. He's become argumentative. Linda was wondering if this was a sign of dementia or something else going on. Though Laurie couldn't provide anything definitive without meeting her father and talking to his doctor further, she did provide Linda with this advice:

Before we discuss specific behaviors, this is certainly the piece that a lot of family members need to get a grasp on in order to make it a more manageable situation for everyone. That is to understand that behaviors have a reason and have a cause, and we need to understand what that cause is. I like to say that behaviors are a way of communicating, that when a person is agitated or angry or perhaps refusing to take a bath, that there's usually a reason that that person is exhibiting those behaviors.

If you had some type of dementia and someone was trying to tell you that you needed a bath and if you said, "No, I don't need a bath. I just had a bath," but in reality the timeframe is a little skewed because of your memory loss, it's understandable that you might feel a loss of control, like your privacy is being invaded. You might feel insulted because someone is telling you something that you thought you already did. So when we look at the behaviors, it can help for us to ask ourselves, "What is this person trying to say? What does this person need? What does this person want?" I like to say, "She's not misbehaving, she's communicating."

Oftentimes, we can find why a person may be doing certain things by keeping a log. It's plain detective work. It's trying to solve a problem. If you just look at a situation such as bathing or even anger, describe the behavior, jot down when it occurred and where it occurred and who was around, then put down something you tried and to see if it works. Now, we know that this often isn't a simple puzzle to solve, but sometimes by jotting down just those few things can allow us to take a deeper look into a behavior and to see if there's a possible trigger that we have overlooked. That can often provide some answers.

Two of the most difficult and complex behaviors that family caregivers have to deal with are anger and aggression. The starting point is always to see if there are any possible physical, medical, or emotional causes of those behaviors. Now, whether the brain changes from dementia directly cause agitation may not be totally understood but it surely is a possibility.

Another physical cause perhaps would be medication. Medication changes or side effects that can cause agitation or anxiety. We know that if we don't feel well, if we're in pain, if we have a physical illness, we might get anxious or agitated, but if we don't have the ability to tell someone that, how we're feeling, we have a headache or our stomach hurts, then sometimes we can be more restless, we can pace, we can get angry, our mood changes, and it can be very hard for people to figure this out.

Untreated depression can cause anger. I think what is really important to understand is that oftentimes anger is a major symptom of depression, but we don't usually think about that. We usually think about someone who's depressed as being sad or maybe melancholy. There are many other possible causes of agitation, anxiety, anger, and aggression. If we look at some of the things to do for that, the first place to start is to call the doctor and request an evaluation to see if there are any physical causes to a person's shift in behavior, including an evaluation for depression, and to make sure that pain is treated adequately.

Also, to note is that when people spend a lot of time in a chair or in a wheelchair, it can be very uncomfortable and can cause pain. It's important to get that person up and moving so that it's not so painful and to get them to move around a regular basis. Just imagine, if you or I were sitting on a chair for four hours, how it would be to get up after that length of time. Stretching can be really helpful. There are many, many more things that we can do in response to possible physical, medical and emotional causes of what we call the four A's: agitation, anxiety, anger, and aggres-

sion. There are also things that can go on around the person, around the place where the person is.

There could be sensory overload. There's too much going on. There are too many people, there's too much noise, there are too many distractions, and when they feel overwhelmed, oftentimes they can feel angry and they can lash out either physically or verbally because that's the only way they can tell someone, "I can't tolerate this anymore." That includes television or radio that is too loud — that may not be understood. We often hear from family members talk about the relative watching television and not being able to distinguish if it's reality or if it's on television and if they're watching some action thriller or the news that is describing some violent events, then we can understand the impact on a person's behavior and their mood.

We really have to evaluate the environment and to see if it's conducive to a person. Calm, not too quiet but not too stimulating. Oftentimes, that is trial by error to find out what is the right environment so someone can feel in control and calm and content.

One of the suggestions that I make to family members when their relative is experiencing some changes and they're not quite sure what could be going on, the first place to go is to the doctor, and to just write a very short note to the doctor describing what is going on and to either email that to the doctor ahead of the appointment or hand it in at the time of the appointment so the doctor has a chance to read it before coming to the examining room. That gives the doctor a little background information, but it's also the most respectful thing to do for someone who has dementia so that we're not talking about the person in front of her. This is really very true if the person with dementia is not an accurate reporter.

However, people in the earlier stages who may be able to self-report how they're feeling and where the pain is and how it's changed for them, and then they should address these concerns directly with the doctor. The doctor has the whole picture to determine how he or she is going to treat some of the symptoms.

Though it is important for Linda to get a doctor's advice as it relates to her father's behaviors, many people with dementia will act perfectly fine when visiting with the doctor. For Linda, having a description of the situations and behaviors associated with those situations will help the doctor determine the next best steps. Medication is not always the answer and incorrect medication could make the situation worse.

TIPS FOR COMMUNICATING WITH SOMEONE WITH DEMENTIA

Our earliest memories stay with us the longest, so instead of asking, "Did you like the movie you saw last week?" we might ask about a childhood friend.

For Linda, her brother, and sister, keeping up with, let alone understanding, their parents' behavioral changes can be frustrating and confusing. But caregivers can be part of the problem, by fighting against their relative's dementia, or they can be part of the solution, by working with their relative's changing self.

Laurie White shared some communication strategies for Linda for helping to make life easier for her and her family:

1. *Recognize that people with dementia have the same needs we do. Those basic needs are to be loved, to feel productive, to feel a sense of belonging, and to be comfortable.*

2. *Don't label people by their symptoms. We all want to be acknowledged as who we are, not by a symptom we have, whether it's arthritis, diabetes, or dementia. For instance, instead of calling people who wander "Wanderers," we can describe them as someone who might pace or walk away or need exercise. This can really change our attitude toward the person with dementia.*

3. ***Let go of the need to be right.*** *Family members, especially spouses, tend to fall into back-and-forth banter patterns: "When we took our European trip five years ago..." "No, we didn't take that trip five years ago; we took it eight years ago." This doesn't work with someone with memory loss. And the bottom line is: does it really make any difference? No. Let it go.*

4. ***Include them.*** *Include our loved one in our conversations. Think of it as talking with our relative, not talking to our relative. Sometimes they confabulate, that is, make up facts or stories, because they want to be a part of the conversation. Resist the urge to say, "No Mom, that's not right." Again, is it really important if the facts are straight?*

5. ***Acknowledge.*** *Even when we don't understand what someone is saying, we can say something as simple as, "That's interesting," "Thanks for sharing that with me," or "I didn't know that." It all comes back to the human need to be acknowledged.*

6. ***Remember that they forget.*** *In our everyday conversation, we might say, "Do you remember when..." and "Do you remember that person..." For someone with memory loss, that's not the best way to start a conversation, because chances are they don't remember. Also, a person's long-term memory stays with them much longer than the short term. Our earliest memories stay*

with us the longest, so instead of asking, "Did you like the movie you saw last week?" we might ask about a childhood friend. Instead of asking open-ended questions like, "Hey, Mom, who is this in the picture?" we can prompt them with, "Isn't this a picture of you?" This way we are not calling upon the person to remember. We are providing some details up front.

7. **Don't argue.** Even if your mom says that vase of flowers is an accordion, don't argue. You'll never win an argument with someone with dementia because if that's their reality — if that's what they firmly believe and it's not a safety threat — then is it really worth arguing about? No. Just go with it.

8. *Apologize.* If we or someone else does something that upsets the loved one, we can acknowledge that they are upset, and apologize even if it wasn't our fault. Just saying, "I'm sorry" or "I'm sorry you're feeling that way," and maybe staying with them, stroking their arm, or walking with them might help defuse the situation.

9. *Seek support.* Most of us didn't train to become caregivers; we were thrown into the role. That's why it's crucial that we connect with other caregivers and professionals to learn what we can do now and how we can prepare for the future as our loved one's dementia progresses. We need a support group. Our well-being and that of our loved one depend on it.

Though Linda is doing her best to communicate with her parents, she has to make a conscious effort not to correct or disagree with her parents because they are not remembering. It would be like me saying to you, "You're not reading this book right now." You would want to correct me, but if I were the person with dementia, I might truly believe you are not reading the book. Linda and her siblings must be in the moment of her parents, because there is no good to come from telling them something different than how their parents see things right now.

FAMILY FIGHTS ABOUT AGING PARENTS

The subjects of money and care are the two areas that cause the greatest amount of conflicts among families as it relates to caring for their aging parents. I'd like to introduce two mediation experts in this area and share a conversation they had with me and Linda regarding her family's situation. I set up a conference call for Linda to speak to both Carolyn and Mikol to discuss how these experts work with families regarding conflicts having to do with their parents.

Carolyn Rosenblatt is a registered nurse with ten years of nursing and 27 years of experience as a practicing attorney. She has extensive, hands-on experience in elderly care, aging parents, and working with caregivers. She is an experienced mediator helping to resolve family conflicts since 2006.

Dr. Mikol Davis is a Clinical Psychologist with over 38 years as a Mental Health Provider. He has worked with many families and is an expert in aging issues. He is also an experienced mediator of many kinds of family disputes, and often works with Carolyn to resolve them.

Linda, her father, and her siblings are not agreeing on several issues and how money should be spent for their care. Also, Linda is feeling resentment towards her brother and sister because the burden is falling on her to take care of the present situation and future plans of their parents. Linda is having her own family and work issues and the responsibilities have become overwhelming.

Mikol: It's important to really understand the nature of the conflict. Often it involves interviewing different family members and finding out that generally what's driving the conflict is frequently something that has been going on for years and years.

So, the conflict is usually not fresh. It's something that has been harbored as a part of the whole family structure, whether the oldest sibling adult child is going to decide how things are going to go down, or it's the one that has more influence over the parent. Often, it's the adult child that lives closest to the parents that feels that they're more involved and more knowledgeable about the extent of what their aging parent needs.

So, the first step is to understand the politics around the conflict and to be sensitive to the fact that generally what you're doing is waiting in a situation that has been going on for years in terms of the underlying feud between siblings or between conflicts between adult children and the parents. We really work to understand the nature of what we're dealing with, which is often historically driven. Once we do that (and we're able to do that fairly quickly, because of the many families that we've served), we know how to cut to the chase once we discover what is the underlying conflict.

Then we focus on seeing if we can help the various members of the family and make some agreements about the rules of the road going forward. Often one of those rules is that the focus is on making decisions about mom or dad and it's not about the past.

A good agreement is "Let's focus on the present and not rehash a history lesson of what you did when I was 13". As soon as we can begin to establish some semblance of rules, that's an excellent start. From there, you know what we're really shooting for is to determine what realistically can be accomplished within the scope of our mediating or having a family meeting.

And that's what the next step is — to look at realistic expectations of either what the individual family members need, or as outsiders, providing some direction on things that we see that are imminent that need to be addressed.

Carolyn: I think that decision-making independence is also a big issue. I think that most adult children want to honor their parents' independence and those parents definitely don't want to lose control of their lives. They see giving up any form of their independence as a step toward losing control, which is quite terrifying.

There can be conflict over decision-making even if the parent is competent; maybe they are physically infirm or getting that way. And the adult children want them to have help at home, for instance.

Maybe the parents don't want it, though they really need it and everybody else thinks they need it. They don't think they need it so there are arguments about that. And, you know, we have that issue in our own lives right now with Mikol's mom, who just turned 92, lives by herself and still drives. She lives hundreds of miles away from us, is very independent, very stubborn, and it's time for her to get some help at home. She's having trouble walking but her mind is very sharp.

So, you know it's a bit of a struggle to try to get her to even accept using a wheelchair when we're going to be walking *for a long way because she just can't do it. And we'll probably get resistance but I think she's at a point where she may relent. Some parents do not, they just don't. And this fight goes on until there's a crisis.*

Mikol: And that, I think, is universal because people are fighting to maintain their independence. Accepting that they need help means that they're one step in the grave and they don't want to accept that. I think it's a real struggle for the adult child to be able to deal with that level of stubbornness, knowing that your aging loved one is basically making decisions where they're going to be at increased risk for a fall or other kind of danger. But unfortunately, stubbornness continually gets in the way as it has with my 92 year-old mom.

But we've got some different angles that we've been trying and some seem to be pretty effective. And I think the one that is usually most effective is the one when we talk about, you know, "This is not for you, Mom, it's for us. It's really for our peace of mind. It's for our ability to sleep at night and know that there's someone there." "Do it for me mom" seems to be pretty effective.

Linda brought up that she doesn't believe her brother would participate in this type of mediation. She asked Mikol or Carolyn to comment on how that type of situation could be handled in regards to her siblings.

Mikol: What we wind up doing is providing a lot of information and somewhat coaching of the family members who do want to come to the table so to speak. We talk about how to deal with the one or two members of the family who are dragging their feet and don't want to be involved.

So, that's really effective because often what we'll do is have people come to us and we'll tell them that unless we can get everybody involved, it likely won't be effective; and sometimes it's the situation where it's clear that the family has got to identify that there are going to be primary decision makers, since the decisions have got to be made.

If certain family members just want to drag their heels to not participate, that's their choice, but they can be provided with the information on the decisions that are going to be made and how it's going to impact them going forward, and that seems to be an effective strategy.

Carolyn: Then we have the issue of power of attorney. The legal document gives the person full authority. If they've got power of attorney and it's unlimited, they can do whatever they want. But, one of the things I try to help people understand is, you may have legal authority, but if you do not want to trash your sibling relationships for the rest of your lives, it might be a good idea to include other people in the decision-making process to at least invite them to offer an opinion; "Will you agree with it or not?" And see if you can respectfully allow them to weigh in, since it's their parent, too.

That works sometimes with people who are emotionally mature enough to do it, but, as Mikol said, these conflicts often emerge appearing to be about the care of mom or dad, appearing to be about the money, appearing to be about who's doing more work than someone else, but they're really about historic conflicts that go back much farther and they act them out in the guise of being about the problem at the moment.

What we try to do is make sure that we encourage people to reach agreements. This is not therapy when we're doing family mediations. We're not going to fix all those old wounds and we encourage them to just stay in the present. What we can do right now is focus on making life better for mom and dad now, for the next month, until the end of their life, whatever it is, and if we can keep them focused on that and try to be respectful and open, that helps.

Another thing that helps is when it comes to the money; I've encouraged and informed a lot of people with power of attorney that they have an obligation to let everybody know how the money is being spent. Okay, you're spending it on the caregiver, so you're spending it on whatever you need for your parent, but keep records, be transparent, share that with everybody, email it to them; let them all have access to the records, so that you don't make people suspicious because that quality of being suspicious about money is quite common.

Linda said she wasn't comfortable with her brother from the standpoint that she doesn't want to spend their parents' money if their dad says that he can take care of their mom. Though Linda's brother knows that money is going to go to their mom or dad's care, if too much is spent on their care, then he will inherit less at the end of their lives. The big concern is if dad agrees to give Linda's brother the power of attorney, she feels that will be the worst case scenario relative to their care.

Carolyn: Yeah, that's very problematic. There's a certain greed factor, you know. What it boils down to very bluntly is, if you spend money taking care of mom or dad and paying caregivers or paying for assisted living, or paying for whatever it is they need, I'm not going to inherit what's mine... that is greed! And it's really very distressing to see it.

What we do to address that is to remind them that the parent does not owe them an inheritance, and that the inheritance they're expecting is not theirs until the parent is gone. And it is not appropriate or fair and in fact, it might even be abusive to withhold what the parent needs, so that it can be saved to give to the kids.

And the ironic twist in this is that aging parents, like Linda's parents, often have no concept of how expensive it's going to be to pay for long-term care, in whatever form it takes. They're not prepared and they didn't plan on it. They didn't think they'd live this long and they didn't know how much it's going to cost. People are living longer, and longer, and longer. It's great except that when they become infirm, nobody has any idea how they're going to cover the cost.

So, we just try to straighten them out on what the priorities are. We're very respectful in the way we do that, but you know, it is really the parent's money. We remind them of that — they don't have a right to it and that the parent definitely has the right to be properly cared for as they become less able to care for themselves.

To sum it up, we urge you to have a family meeting and to start making some plans, especially with a parent who has any kind of physical difficulty seems to be showing signs of memory loss — which can be the lead-in to dementia.

Memory loss does not necessarily mean you're going to develop dementia, but it is the first symptom of dementia when somebody is going to get it. And it's a caregiving burden, to put it bluntly.

Families need to take the time and get past their internal turmoil and start thinking about how they're going to care of their loved ones. This parent who needs help is going to need more over time. And the family needs to figure out how they're going to pay for it.

Is everyone going to pitch in? Is the family home going to be sold to pay for care? Are they going to liquidate whatever assets the parent has? Do they have a choice? Can they keep the parent out of a nursing home? Is there a way to manage enough combinations of help with family members or caregivers who are paid to supplement that, to enable the parent to stay at home?

Mikol: Also, if you're not going to step up and be proactive and deal with something that most of us don't want to deal with, then the options available will be forced upon you... and they are few and far between.

Carolyn: There's usually one leader in the family. That person needs to suggest the family meeting. If people don't get along you can do the meeting by telephone. You can also communicate by email. But the point is to communicate. If you struggle with your other family members and don't get along, you know it's going to be difficult and you should get a third party talking to everyone.

After the call with Mikol and Carolyn, Linda decided that she would handle family communication by writing out what she thought a good plan would be for being proactive about caring for her parents. Then she talked to her parents about it and emailed the plan to her siblings, inviting them all to discuss the issues with her.

Even with the resistance she encountered, she was able to move things toward greater awareness, and to get a sense of where everyone stood.

MANAGING YOUR PARENTS' MONEY

Linda's father still handles the bills and when she was recently at their home, she noticed that there were unopened envelopes of unpaid bills. It wasn't due to lack of money in their account; the bills just weren't getting paid. She reviewed her parent's bank statements and saw checks going out to people for things that her father couldn't even explain. On top of that, she saw checks for thousands of dollars to her brother. Though her father wrote the checks, she was concerned that her own brother was taking financial advantage of her parents. After discussing the situation with me, I suggested that she meet with an expert in this field, Erik Aho.

Erik's career spans over 25 years of accounting and legal experience. He provides forensic accounting services, focusing on business fraud and embezzlement, fiduciary misconduct, and elder financial abuse. I explained what Linda learned at her recent visit to her parents. I asked Erik to talk more about forensic accounting, elder financial abuse, and how he may be able to assist Linda.

When Linda expressed alarm at the thought that what her brother was doing might be termed embezzlement, I reassured her that at this stage what she most needed was good information about issues involving misuse of elderly parents' finances, in case that possibility with her brother turned out to be true. She needed support if this was the case.

Here's what Erik said about this issue:

Forensic accounting is about being a fraud examiner. That's essentially what I do. I conduct fraud examinations, so I'm looking at financial statements, bank accounts, and financial activity. I'm looking to see whether or not there may have been a theft or embezzlement or misappropriation of funds. In the case of subsequent civil or criminal actions, my findings might be used as the form of evidence to determine whether or not some theft or embezzlements may have occurred. In other words, to sum it up, I'm kind of a glorified dumpster diver.

As far as elder financial abuse, it has always been with us but it has only within, I would say, the last 10 to 15 years that states have recognized this as a separate crime. The reason for doing so is multifold. But certainly one of the reasons is that when an elder suffers a financial loss from a con artist or something similar, it can be very difficult, if not impossible, for the elder to recover financially. They're on a fixed income, there's not going to be additional income coming in, they can't just pick up another job. So, once they're victimized financially, it's very, very difficult for the elder to recover. And I would even add that there's studies that have been performed that indicate an elder who has suffered from financial abuse lives a shorter life. Their lifespan is shortened. You can almost make the argument that elder financial abuse is a crime against a person in the sense that it can basically kill them. That's the blunt way of putting it. But the consequences can be severe.

Linda approached her father with an offer of handling the payments for all of their expenses, but he didn't want to hear of it. I asked Erik how he suggests handling this type of situation, since it's quite clear that Linda's father does not want to give up his independence; yet we have issues going on that could be fraud.

I think the most difficult problem that a son or daughter may face in trying to manage a parent's finances, is not the accounting aspect. In fact, I teach sons and daughters and family members how to manage parents' finances. I can say the accounting side of it is fairly easy to teach... I can do that. The more difficult aspect is not the management, it's the communication. We hear a lot of advice given to just ask open-ended questions, just listen, if the elder should depart from the topic you are discussing, go ahead and wait. That's all good advice, it makes perfect sense. The problem with that, however, is that it doesn't put it in context. It doesn't explain why you should do these things. So, let me explain very briefly what I believe an elder is going through in this type of situation.

First of all, an elder is faced with issues of purpose and issues of control. At the later stage of your life, you're attempting to slice and dice and put it all together, figure out what is the purpose of your life. What does this all mean? Some people talk in terms of legacy, I talk about in terms of purpose. But as an elder tries to determine what their life meant and what episodes in their life might mean, they're unwilling to give up control. They want control over certain aspects of their life, whether it be finances or something as simple as driving. They need to control these aspects in their lives so they can make sense of what their life meant or what it continues to mean.

I can give you a perfect example. My mother, who passed away in 2010, for years struggled with the bad relationship that she had with her father. I would hear the stories over and over again, very repetitive. What I didn't understand at that time, but began to realize later, was that she was trying to ascribe a certain meaning or significance to her poor relationship with her father, what it meant to her life and how she could recover from that. It wasn't until two days before she passed away when she told me that she had forgiven her father.

Now, in terms of her legacy, what her life meant to her, a large part of that was the relationship she had with her father. The fact that she could forgive him at that very late stage meant that she could give up control on that issue. That is what I think is really important. If you as a son or daughter are attempting to manage parents' finances, and they're resisting, — well, you know the story.

It's not a question of balancing their checking account, it's a matter of whether or not your parent is willing to let you do that. So, it's important to understand what they may be thinking in terms of purpose in their life and how that relates to whether or not they're going to give up control so that you could help them. And we can talk about that in length. But anyway, this gives you a brief understanding of what an elder may be going through, and it may assist the son or daughter in approaching the elder.

Again, once you understand the context, you can appreciate why it is important to let the elder talk to let them assemble what they're going to do. By the way, it's not really they're wandering off the topic because they do not understand what it is they need to talk about, it's because they're trying to make sense of something else and they're doing it in their own way. So, let them do that. Hopefully you want to reach the point where they will allow you to assist them in managing their finances and not have it be an issue of control.

Keep them involved in the process, because at the end of the day, it's their money. It's their finances and their life. Now, how and when you intervene, and to what level, it all depends on their personal circumstance and it's a dynamic target; though there are those who would argue that as you get older, you lose your faculties, and you can't manage your affairs that well. I would challenge that. I would simply say it may be true that a person may be suffering from a cognitive decline and can no longer manage their finances, but it may also be they're looking at their finances in a different way. Remember that ultimately everybody is allowed to make bad decisions. Short of undue influence, or a scam, or dementia, or other cognitive or neurological impairments, parents as well as children are allowed to make bad decisions with their money.

But if it's a question of where there's a clinical reason for mismanagement or if they are victims of a theft or a crime that changes things a little bit. That's where you want to step in. I usually say that at the beginning, if your parent is what I call young-old as opposed to old-old, merely setting the stage for a "systems down the road" is enough. And may mean simply understanding what your parents' expectations are about their retirement or what they want to do with their money.

Maybe that's good enough. Maybe intermediate steps as you go down that road, maybe simply reviewing what their finances are and understanding what their expenditures and income sources are, maybe that's enough. When they reach old-old ,which I define as when a retiree or a senior devotes most attention to their health care issues, maybe actual active management is appropriate.

I think that most sons or daughters have a fairly good understanding of where they and their parents would be on that spectrum. It's important to remember not to jump the gun and do more than what your parents are willing to have you do. Again, we come back to issues of legacy and purpose and control. To sum that up, it's a moving target. It's a very doable kind of thing, but the son or daughter needs to be to be mindful of the process.

The son or daughter can be an additional set of eyes to assist the parent in making decisions. This is really good in terms of reviewing checking accounts, good in terms of consolidating banking accounts, eliminating extra credit cards. You should want an extra set of eyes so you can understand what is happening and that parents don't have to rely entirely on themselves to make decisions and to see what's going on.

If the son or daughter is incapable or simply unwilling to manage finances, they can hire a professional fiduciary. You can certainly use a daily money manager. A daily money manager, as the term implies, manages the daily transactions for an elder or someone else who's incapable of man-

aging their money. You can check out this website at www.
aadmm.com. That's a good start.

After these suggestions by Erik, Linda approached her dad on just assisting him with the bills but not taking over the responsibility. It is quite apparent to Linda that her dad is not capable of doing it himself but is trying to keep him involved in the process.

* * *

Based on this valuable input from our experts, I told Linda she was taking on way too much herself. I suggested to her that prior to talking to or meeting with her siblings, she should share a list of the responsibilities that need to be handled. To make sure that their parents' situation is being handled in an effective way, each sibling can take on certain responsibilities.

Though Linda would be the person meeting with the doctor locally, there are legal matters like the power of attorney and following up with unpaid bills that could be handled by her brother and sister.

Linda realized that she couldn't handle all of this alone while working and taking care of her own family. She knows she needs to get her siblings involved in the process and communicate with them on a regular and scheduled basis.

Linda has also provided some of the resources provided to her and shared them with her siblings, including the Alzheimer's Association, which can be helpful from an education standpoint. They have local chapters where they offer seminars to learn more about their mom's disease and dad's cognitive decline.

CHAPTER TWO

Paying for Long-Term Care

Linda thought that everything was getting paid for, but saw many bills for both her parents' care. Assuming Medicare was paying for all their care, Linda wanted to better understand what her parents' Medicare covers.

I introduced her to Christopher Westfall, who is a licensed insurance agent whose group helps seniors exclusively on the telephone with their Medicare plans. I've asked Chris to go over the basics with Linda about Medicare and differences with Medicaid. I know Linda will have a much better understanding after Chris provides this information to her.

UNDERSTANDING THE INS AND OUTS OF MEDICARE

Medicare is available for seniors over 65 who have earned the benefit. It's not a handout. It's not a free giveaway program. Seniors have earned the right to be on Medicare by having worked 40 quarters or 10 years of full-time work experience through their adult lives. That is a benefit that they've earned and it generally pays 80% of all their doctor and hospital and x-rays and labs and so forth when they turn 65.

The only question then, now you've got Medicare, which is a wonderful benefit, is what are you going to do for the other 20%? There's no limit on how much you could pay out of your pocket for that 20%, so seniors have two choices. They can either do a Medicare Supplement which supplements that 80% to pay the difference, or they completely abdicate their healthcare to an HMO — typically, a Medicare Advantage plan — and, by doing so, they pull out of the Medicare system and turn their healthcare over to a managed network where the focus is on saving money.

On the Medicare Advantage plan, the senior has a network of doctors. There are restrictions on them, and they've got a maximum out-of-pocket. The average now is $6700 every year that they could be forced to pay out of their pocket before the health plan pays for everything. They go into the hospital and those plans and it could be $200 or $300 per day in the hospital, but, most importantly, on an "Advantage" plan, which is not really an advantage in that it's the HMO or the medical plan then that decides what healthcare you get.

If your doctor thinks you need an MRI, CAT scan and an x-ray, that HMO Medicare Advantage plan may say "Well, we're focused on cost" because they are, that's their mission, to save money. Let's just start with an x-ray and see if we can get it done there. Well, your doctor may say look we're looking at three different things. We need to see three different angles. The managed care plan, that Medicare Advantage plan, again having replaced all of Medicare, limits them to what the health plan will approve.

If you're on Medicare Advantage, you've got an insurance company that's taking money from the government to manage your care for you. On the other side of the fence, where I spend most of my focus, is on the Medicare supplement side. They are free to go to any doctor in the country, any healthcare facility, any provider. Suppose they get a brain tumor and they want to go to MD Anderson Cancer treatment center in Texas — they pick up the phone, they make a call. If they want to go to chance or Arnold Palmer Hospital or any specialty facility in the country, they can do that. They just have to arrange their travel and set an appointment, but it's paid for. The senior is still in control of their healthcare.

You can't have both the Medicare Advantage and the Medicare Supplement. It's one or the other. One of them cost money. The Medicare Supplement has a monthly fixed premium and that can adjust every year. Sometimes *they go down, but most of the time, they go up. It's usually around $100, $150 maximum for a Medicare supplement plan. On the Medicare Advantage side, many times there is no monthly premium.*

Well, if you're not paying any premium at all and the insurance company is getting paid by the government to manage your healthcare, you have to wonder where is the money coming from and what kind of care am I going to receive and, like I said, you pay as you go on those plans. If you go onto the hospital on a Medicare Advantage plan, you could be coming out of the hospital with a $1,600, $1,800 or $2,000 bill because you pay as you go with those plans. So a typical senior on a fixed income can be shocked to find that they come out of a hospital situation with a $2,000 bill and if they're readmitted, it's even worse, and they could be paying that whole thing all over again. That's why I think the Medicare Supplements are better way to go. You got a fixed cost with no surprises. You just continue to pay your monthly premium and it's guaranteed renewable for the rest of your life.

Linda now understands why she is seeing bills for her parents' care, but wants to review the choices to lessen their costs. I asked Chris to explain Medigap which could be a good option for her parents:

That's the government's interesting term that they've affixed to Medicare supplements. All the same thing, it just fills in the gap between what original Medicare pays and what the doctor has billed. It fills in the gap. It's the same term as Medicare Supplement. The Medigap plans, (that's what the Medicare in your guidebook calls it). Again, when you're turning 65, you've got the world as your oyster. You can pick any of those Medicare Supplement plans with no health underwriting at all. You just merely pick the best plan in the market for you and that's what we focus on.

Later if you want to change the plan on the Medicare Supplement side, you have to qualify by answering some health questions. There's the physical exam, just answering health questions. Conversely, on the Medicare Advantage side, you can sign up for those plans once per year and there are no health questions at all, which again begs the question if it's open to anybody and there is no screening whatsoever, what kind of folks are they going to get? They're going to get anybody and everybody. Sick or not, and you benefit or suffer based on the fact that you're in a pool of healthy or sick people. That's how they adjust their benefits year-to-year.

With the Medicare Advantage plan, you can switch those plans and as they are one-year contracts. Every year, they change. The copayments change, the networks change, the doctors change. They all change those things once per year whereas the Medigap or the Medicare supplement stays con-

sistent. When you buy that Medicare Supplement contract, it's going to be that same benefit plan for the rest of your life. You are in control of that plan. You can leave anytime you want. The company cannot arbitrarily say, "Oh by the way we're going to double your cost when you go to the doctor" or "We're going to double your cost when you go to the hospital". This has happened often recently on Medicare Advantage plans in response to the Affordable Care Act.

Though Linda's parents are already on Medicare, she was wondering how the process works to get them onto a Medicare Supplement and how she would sign up when ready.

You should start that process right before turning 65. Now you can apply for a Medigap plan up to six months before you turn 65, and you know Medicare itself is going to kick in when you're 65. One nice little tactic that we try to employ when we can is there someone looking at the six months out from turning 65, we could literally write an application today six months out and lock in that rate and that benefit plan to so that when they do turn 65, they had a rate that was good six months ago and that rate is locked in for an additional year on those Medicare Supplement or Medigap plans. That's a good way to go but they could wait. We just don't want to wait six months past turning 65 or else you lose that window of guaranteed issue ability to get a Medicare supplement plan with no questions asked.

Medicare Supplement companies are just like cable compa-
nies and cell phone providers that often give a better rate for
somebody coming in brand-new than they do for their loyal
customers that have been with them for five years. So, to
keep them on their toes, it's always good to have your agent
shop the plans for you at least every year or two. That's what
we do with our clients.

QUALIFYING FOR MEDICAID BENEFITS

Though Linda would prefer her parents living in an
assisted living community with memory care for her
mother, the costs may not be affordable for the family. She
needs to understand the process for getting her parents
qualified for Medicaid. Generally speaking, Medicare
is health and hospitalization insurance and Medicaid is
more like long-term care insurance in a medical setting,
such as hospitals and skilled nursing facilities.

We spoke to Roy Litherland, an attorney whose practice
emphasizes special needs and estate planning. In addition, in his extensive legal background, Roy was also previously licensed as a certified public accountant. I asked
Roy to give us an overview of the differences between
Medicare and Medicaid.

There is a lot of confusion about that. I'll take just a minute
to distinguish between Medicare and Medicaid. Medicare

is a federal statute, and its primary function is to allow people over age 65 to be able to obtain reasonable cost medical insurance. Now, there are other things that it will do, but that's its primary function.

Then there is Medicaid, which is also a federal statute as well as a funding statute. Very simply, when Medicaid, the federal statute passed back in 1965, provided a structure for a public assistance program, and each of the states could elect to participate or not. If they elected to participate, then each participating state would have to pass legislation in conformity with the federal Medicaid structure and, if they did so, then the federal government would fund by transferring money from the federal government down to the state to be used to implement those public assistance programs.

Each state has to pass their own laws to conform to that. In California, that is called Medi-Cal. Medi-Cal is essentially the laws, the regulations, in California that have been enacted in order to conform to the federal Medicaid statute. Each state, if they participate, can in a sense call this program what they want.

First I want to address a common misconception that people have that Medicare is going to pay for their skilled nursing home costs. Now, the reality is that for 98% of all of the people who qualify for Medicare, 98% of them will never qualify to have Medicare pay any of their skilled nursing *home cost. That's going to be limited to about 2% of the entire Medicare population. As to that 2%, what Medicare pays for is very limited.*

Assuming that a person is part of that 2%, then Medicare will pay for the first 20 days of skilled nursing home cost. After that 20 days for the next 80 days the person in the skilled nursing home will pay a deductible of $152 per day, and that number changes annually. Then Medicare will pay the excess. At the end of 100 days, Medicare pays nothing whatsoever, so you are now completely on your own.

We also know that statistically the average stay in a skilled nursing facility is 1.84 years, and so you can see that 100 days of assistance isn't going to really help a lot for most people. Also, here in our area, we're looking at well over $300 per day as a typical cost for skilled nursing facility care. Medicare just isn't going to be a technique for taking care of that.

Now, moving to the issue of whether or not you have to be broke in order to qualify for Medicaid, the answer is that there are a number of assets you can have and still qualify for Medicaid. An example of that would be your personal household effects, one automobile, a cemetery plot, $2,000 worth of non-exempt assets, and that's the number people usually look at, which is, "Oh, I can't have more than $2,000 worth of cash or investments, and if I have *more than that, I can't qualify for Medicaid," and that's true. There is one major asset, however, that you can have and still qualify for Medicaid, and that is the family home, so a person can own their family home and still qualify for Medicaid.*

Now, then the question becomes, "Well, is there any way that we can plan, rearrange our assets in such a fashion as to be able to accelerate my qualification for Medicaid?" and the answer is, "Yes, there are a whole variety of techniques that can be used that would allow a person to shift assets, change his ownership structure, things of that nature, so that they can qualify for Medicaid without essentially dissipating all of their assets."

Linda shared with me that she moved some of her parents' money around into her children's names to show that her parents have less money, thinking that's the easy way to do this. Roy commented strongly on this.

Well, let's talk about that. There's the easy way of doing it, which is almost always criminal. There are people who decide, "Okay, I'm going to take the poor man's approach to this. I'm going to give my assets to my kids. I'm going to apply for Medicaid and when answering the question, 'Have I made any gifts,' I'm going to answer, 'No.'"

I find that to be a very shortsighted approach given the fact that there are so many techniques whereby you can achieve the same goal and do it within the confines of the rules, the regulations of Medicaid, and do it perfectly legally. In just transferring the money and lying on the application is certainly something that mystifies me, but I guess that's primarily for people who don't know that there is an alternative.

Medicaid will pay the cost for skilled nursing facility care, but it will not pay for assisted living and smaller residential care homes in most states. Now, I'd like to take just a moment to distinguish between a skilled nursing facility and an assisted living facility.

Legally, a skilled nursing facility has to have a licensed doctor or a licensed registered nurse on staff 24 hours a day, seven days a week. The difference between a skilled nursing facility and the assisted living facility is that the assisted living facility does not have that kind of person involved.

The reason I mention that is because you can have facilities where you have one building and this wing over here is skilled nursing facility, and this wing over here is an assisted living facility, and, but for the fact that over in this wing you have a registered nurse wandering around, there's essentially no difference between the level of care that's being provided or even the facilities.

I need to address the issue of mental capacity. Let's face it. There are a number of people, a lot of people who are in a skilled nursing facility because they have lost mental capac-

ity. They can't stay at home by themselves any longer. It would be dangerous for them to do so. They actually can't be, for instance, in assisted living facility because of their lack of mental capacity. They need more attention, more assistance than they would get in an assisted living facility.

The problem is that we can do an awful lot of rearranging of a person's assets in order to qualify for Medicaid. However, they need to have mental capacity to be able to do it. For instance, someone who lacks mental capacity can't sign a deed giving away their home to their children to avoid the Medicaid recovery lien or to be able to make gifts in such a fashion to reduce their non-exempt assets below $2,000.

The heartbreak is that if someone lacks mental capacity and they really need to rearrange their assets in order to qualify for Medicaid to preserve limited assets for their needs that are not going to be provided by the Medicaid system, but they lack mental capacity and can't do it. This is why I recommend to Linda and her family not to wait too long.

That addresses the problem of appropriate pre-planning. By that I mean if a person has a very comprehensive estate plan that includes provisions that would allow the family to do Medicaid planning for them in the event of incapacity, then we're okay. I call those provisions "Medicaid triggers." If a person has, for instance, a good durable power of attorney, that includes specific provisions authorizing the *family, the holder of the power of attorney, to do Medicaid planning, now we have the ability to do so.*

Now, without that specific authority, it can create problems. For instance, under the California law, the ability to gift your principal's assets away is never and cannot be implied in a durable power of attorney. In order for a holder of a durable power of attorney to make gifts in anticipation of or a part of a Medicaid planning strategy there has to be the specific authority in it allowing them to make gifts.

Just as important, most of the time gifting authority in a power of attorney is usually limited to whatever the Federal gift tax exemption amount is on an annual basis, which is right now $14,000. Well, that's a huge limitation that doesn't do us any good.

In addition, let's pretend that we have gifting authority and there is no such limitation. Then the question is, can we interpret that document to permit the holder of the power of attorney agency to gift away all of their principal's assets, thereby impoverishing the principal so they no longer have the financial means of providing for themselves. Well, unless there's specific instructions and authority in that document permitting or instructing that to occur, it is highly arguable that doing that is elder abuse, and, as you know, in some states that's a crime.

You need to be very, very careful with making sure that the person's power of attorney document as well as if they have a trust, the trust, contains specific authority granting and instructing that kind of planning to occur.

Knowing we're beginning to see some cognitive decline with Linda's dad, she shouldn't wait too long and begin planning now. He may not be able to be in a position to make those decisions. Roy responded emphatically:

That's exactly correct. Here's a two-minute example. Let's pretend that we have someone who lacks mental capacity and has $600,000 worth of securities, and they have no planning documents. There's nothing I can do to help that person qualify for Medicaid. On the other hand, if that person had a home and no planning documents, I could go to court and probably get a judge to agree to allow us to do something, but if that person who has the $600,000 of securities had proper legal documents, I could show them how very quickly we could move the assets under a Medicaid plan and get them qualified, so pre-planning is extremely important.

HOW LIFE INSURANCE CAN PAY
FOR CARE

Linda shared with me that the family is going to have challenges paying for her parents' care for the long-term. She did tell me that her dad does have a life insurance policy, the very reason I'm having her listen to what Brian May of the Asher Group LLC has to say about life settlements and their ability in negotiating the highest possible offers for their clients' life insurance policies. They accomplish this by using a competitive bid process, and Brian explained how this started and how it all works.

First off, there's a National Underwriter magazine. Back in September 2013, it had kind of an arbitrary thing where it said, "The majority of policy holders let their policy lapse or surrender." So, what does that mean? If you look at the actual individual numbers, like universal policies, which are long term policies, 85 percent did not end up paying death benefits, which is a pretty staggering number. Then you look at term policies, and it's even bigger — that's 95 percent do not end up paying death benefits. In 2012, $662 billion in life insurance benefits, were either lapsed, or surrendered.

I have talked to a lot of insurance agents. I've also talked with lawyers. I've talked to different folks who know seniors, and I would say the vast majority of people have never heard of a life settlement. Simply, a life settlement is the sale of a life insurance policy. Basically the policy owner receives a cash settlement for their policy, and then the investor takes that responsibility over, so that means they actually pay for the premiums for the life of that insurance policy. It's kind of a trade-off. Here's up-front money for your policy, and then we're going to continue paying that, and then that particular investor receives the death benefit at the end.

Why do investors do this? These are not angel investors. They are trying to make a profit, but when it makes sense for both parties involved, the insured, and of course the investor. The main reason that they want to purchase it is because it's a good investment for them. For example, as long as they're going to pay a larger percentage over the cash surrender value, which a lot of policies, not term policies, but universal or whole life have some form of a cash surrender value. For example, if they're able to pay well above and beyond that, then it makes sense. What they would do is they would pay that premium, and at the end, they're going to receive an amount greater than what they put into it. It's an investment for them.

The only caveat to that is if the policy is a term policy, it has to be convertible to a permanent life insurance policy. Typically, that means that's going to be a universal policy. Term policies generally are convertible up to age 75. That doesn't mean every single policy is like that, but, for the most part, 75 years or younger, there is a conversion.

Even though the premium is higher on a conversion, that investor is willing to pay that higher premium. We would never want to put anybody at risk, so we would actually do all the analysis before a person converted that policy. There is an expense to converting that policy as well, but that could be paid out by the life settlement. That way, and I should say this up front, there should be no out of pocket expense for any person when they're doing a life settlement.

One of the greatest challenges many of us in the industry have is when someone needs care, but they don't have the money, and it can get pretty expensive. So I asked Brian to comment on Linda's dad's case. He has a life insurance policy and if the family doesn't have the money to pay for care in the long run, they should not let his policy lapse to save money. But yet, he could sell his policy and get some money to help pay for care.

That's 100 percent correct. To your point, that's exactly what we see, the large majority of the clients need money for long-term care. It's hard to determine how much a person is going to need for care, any kind of care. We see the vast majority of people selling their life insurance policies to pay for that type of service.

A life settlement is not a silver bullet, for lack of a better term, for every situation. In this case, we look at some of the facts and the figures around the large majority of people ending up lapsing or surrendering their policy. If, for example, they're going to lapse or surrender, obviously their family is not going to receive any of that money. We see that the vast majority don't. That's one thing to consider. Also, there is a potential to what they have called a" retained death benefit," meaning that they can get cash for their life insurance policy and still have a portion left back for their family.

It doesn't work in all situations, but that is a possibility. It's not just a policy. They bought it to protect their families, so either if they can't afford it, or in some situations, maybe the kids are grown, and they have enough money now, they've already graduated from college, or maybe it's the spouse has passed away, and that was for the spouse. If circumstances have changed, and they no longer need it, my passion is to make sure A) people know it's a viable option, and B) let them know that they can go ahead and look and see how much money they can get. There's no obligation for life settlement. I should let that be known up front. If a person goes through the process, they receive an offer. They can either accept that offer, or deny that offer. They are not bound to it just because they went through the process.

It's almost like re-insuring again. Just like anybody who applies for insurance, you've got to fill out an application.

You've got to list all your illnesses and previous surgeries, and the doctor reports on all of that. Is that same type of thing that has to be done again? Would Linda's dad have to go through that?

That's a good question. There are no physicals that need to take place. What the investor would like at is a five-year medical history. Through that process — that's something that we would do — we would get five years of medical history, and then they would go through an application process, and then they'd have what's called" independent life expectancy," and a third party would take care of that. With all of that bundled up, that's put before these particular buyers. The buyers have all the information. The reason we're different, is because we're a brokerage form. We don't really care about the investor, we really care about the individual, the senior.

What we do is create a competitive bid process to 20-plus institutional investors. They would look at that policy, and they would have all the same information, and we'd create a competitive bid. Our goal is to get the highest dollar amount for the individual senior.

For example, typically speaking, I use the word typical, because there's no hard fact here, but generally speaking if a person is 70 years or older, and they could be younger if there are significant health problems, it's usually $250,000 or more, that's the benefit amount. For most states, the policy has to have been enforced for at least two years.

I'll give you a real-world experience here. I'm working with a gentleman right now who is 83 years old and he has a larger policy. He has a five-million-dollar policy, but it's a variable universal life. This one's a little bit more technical, because it's actually a security. You don't see a lot of these, these aren't very common, but there's only like a couple of buyers for this, so that's why this example is a little bit different.

This gentleman had $300,000 cash surrender value, and he told his kids, "I can't afford this. If you'd like to continue making the payments you can." They all came back and said, "We can't afford that." We put it up and there were only one or two different buyers for it, but they made an offer of $562,500. He ended up getting $262,500 more than he would have gotten if he'd turned it back in to the insurance company.

As long as the policy is, typically, seven years or older, and the policy is $250,000 dollars or greater, then it's a great case. Again, the nice part is, this is a free evaluation process. What I like to do is I always like to make sure we look through and kind of verify and see if it would be a good fit. The last thing you want to do is waste a person's time.

UNDERSTANDING LONG-TERM CARE INSURANCE

Now that Linda is realizing the costs and challenges of paying for long-term care, I have suggested that she consider long-term care insurance for herself and her husband, and that she speak with Leslie Whiting, a veteran in the long-term care insurance industry. Insurance was the last thing Linda wanted to add to her budget, but she was willing to hear Leslie's overview of the benefits and then make a more informed decision.

Regarding coverage, there does seem to be a misconception by some that Medicare and Medicaid will take care of most long-term care needs. Here are the facts:

1. *Most private health insurance plans follow the same general rules as Medicare. If any long-term care is covered, it is usually for only skilled, short-term and medically necessary care.*

2. *Home care is limited only to medically necessary skilled care. Non-medical homecare, aka custodial or personal care is not covered by health insurance.*

3. *Currently, the coverage in a Skilled Nursing Facility must follow a hospital stay and is limited up to 100 days. If you meet Medicaid's financial eligibility status, you must select a Skilled Nursing Facility that accepts Medicaid.*

Another option is utilizing your own assets, which most of us would want to do in order to maintain our independence. If this were a consideration, it would be important to know the costs (based on today's dollar).

Leslie shared with Linda some median costs of various types of services, using Genworth's 2015 Cost of Care Survey as a source:

- *In-Home Services (Assistance with Activities of Daily Living, including dressing, personal hygiene, bathing, etc.) — $44,616 annually (based on 44 hours/week for 52 weeks)*

- *Assisted Living — $43,200 annually (private/one-bedroom)*

- *Nursing Homes — $80,300 (semi-private) and $90,250 (private) annually*

Leslie went on to talk with Linda about the risks involved with making a decision about long-term care insurance.

Long-term care is not some distant chance that happens to an unfortunate few; rather it is a result of living in a body that does not die quickly. Yes, really difficult things happen, like Alzheimer's Disease or disability from a stroke. Here are some statistics to be aware of:

- *About 70% of individuals over age 65 will require at least some type of long-term care services during their lifetime (U.S. Department of Health and Human Services)*

- *Between 2010 and 2030, the age 75-84 group will increase by more than 86%, the age 85+ group by 57%, and the overall age 75+ group by 77% (U.S. Census Bureau)*

- *Between 2000 and 2010, the death rate for Alzheimer's Disease increased by 39%, whereas death rates for other major causes decreased including Stroke (-36%), Heart disease (-31%), and Cancer (-32%). (Centers for Disease Control and Prevention)*

Unless medically necessary, you can avoid skilled nursing facilities by residing at assisted living facilities, residential care homes or at a home with the needed in-home care. Long-term care insurance makes it much easier to cope with most otherwise uncovered health issues as you get older. Long-term care Insurance could be the best investment one can make.

Long-term care Insurance should be as important as your health care insurance, life insurance, homeowners insurance and even auto insurance. As a matter of fact, following are some well-documented odds comparing the need for long-term care to other occurrences:

- *Odds of Your Home Having a Fire: 1 in 1,200*

- *Odds of Your Auto Being Totaled: 5 in 1,200*

- *Odds of Being Hospitalized: 105 in 1,200*

- *Odds of Needing Long-term care: 720 in 1,200*

Generally, long-term care is needed for conditions that cannot be cured or healed, and for helping people with routine activities such as dressing, bathing, transferring, continence care, toileting and eating. Long-term care Insurance extends for a long period of time, covering care for various types of dementia, including Alzheimer's disease. Long-term care Insurance, which can reduce the burden from your family and your peace of mind, should be a very serious consideration.

Linda and her husband both did decide to apply for the long-term care coverage and receive some quotes before making a final decision. If anything, this could be a great Christmas present for her kids.

LONG-TERM CARE BENEFITS TO VETERAN'S/SPOUSES

Linda's father was a veteran and said she had sent in the application to the Veteran's Administration to get her parents some benefits. They've been waiting for over a year. I explained to her that it is always best to get proper advice before sending in the application, because of how VA benefits work.

That is why I introduced Linda to Victoria Collier, who founded the elder and disability law firm of Victoria L. Collier PC to serve the legal needs of senior citizens when their healthcare needs increase. Victoria explained what her firm specializes in and also discussed how they assist families with the application process and securing benefits for long-term care.

Elder law is like a sister type of law to estate planning. When I give presentations to the community, I'll ask the crowd, "How many of you have heard of elder law attorneys?" Maybe a third of the crowd will raise their hands. When I then say, "How many of you have heard of estate planning?" The entire room raises their hands. What is the difference and what's the commonality? Estate planning essentially draft wills, powers of attorney, and trust. Elder law, we draft wills, powers of attorney, and trust.

However, it's the question and the focus that's being asked as to what makes the difference between the two and so an estate-planning attorney asks the question, "What do you want to do with your stuff when you die?" An elder law attorney asks the question, "What are we going to do if you keep living? How are we going to pay for long-term care?

How are we going to take care of you?" Elder law focuses on quality of life while we're alive and how are we going to use our own resources as well as the other resources available to help pay for long-term care. One of those resources available maybe Medicaid, and one of those resources maybe veterans benefits, which we're talking about today, and then the list goes on.

The VA program I am going to review is not publicized too much. The VA is not essentially putting any resources into mailing veterans letters saying, "Now that you are of an aging population you may need help with care". The VA doesn't have a campaign like that. Instead, they're pulling their resources to change the laws and make it actually harder for veterans to even access this benefit when they do find out it exists.

Essentially there are three main types of veteran's benefits. The first type, which we won't really go into a whole lot, but is relevant, is when someone is injured in the military or because of their military service, there's a compensation. A program where they are compensated with money to help offset those harms that they received because of their military service. That's called service connected disability claims.

Another type of military veterans' benefit is through the healthcare system. If you served a certain period of time and you have an honorable discharge, then you may be able to get healthcare through the Veterans Administration healthcare system.

The one we all going to talk about is that third benefit. That type that no one knows about and that's the veterans improved pension for wartime veterans. Most commonly on the street it's called Aid and Attendance.

The basic eligibility for the pension program has three criteria. The first is the military criteria. We have to have a veteran that served on active duty at least 90 days with one of those days being during a war time period. An example I would give in community presentations is "Tell me when World War II ended" and everybody in the room is very happy and they say, in 1945 and I smiled a little bit and I asked, "Why do you believe that?" Because that's when the New York Times and the Wall Street Journal and everybody had the picture that said, the second A-bomb finished the war.

Unfortunately, that's not when the war ended. It was actually established by Congress to be December 31, 1946. A whole year after 1945. Why that's relevant is that when we do ask our clients or the community, "Are you a wartime veteran?" if they believe the war ended in 1945 and they actually enlisted or were commissioned in any time during 1946, they might answer no and so they might be leaving all money on the table to help pay for care. They have to *have been on active duty at least 90 days, one of which was during the wartime period, which was established by Congress.*

They had to have been discharged with something greater than a dishonorable discharge. Once they've met the military criteria, then there's also healthcare criteria as well as financial criteria.

I have made a mistake in my practice in that when I have asked on the phone when we're trying to associate to somebody the veteran, and I have a female caller. I said, "Was your husband a veteran?" She said, "No, but I was." They recognized that women are veterans, too. I am one of them.

For veterans who served in war time period and are married, if the veteran dies and they were married at least to one year prior to death, the surviving spouse — when they meet all the medical and financial criteria — can receive income to help offset care.

There's an example of a widow of a veteran who needs the assistance of another person to help with at least two activities of daily living on a regular basis. Currently, the widow can receive up to $1,149 of tax-free income per month to help pay for home healthcare, assistant living care, or nursing home care — such as over $13,000 per year. Whereas, a veteran who's married can get just over $25,000 a year, or a single veteran can get just over $21,000 to help pay for those cost.

It would be the same for both veteran and the widow and, ultimately, once we've established the military criteria, we have to determine if they meet the medical criteria.

There are actually three tiers of the benefit. There's the what's called the low-income pension, the base, then one other. All we have to do to qualify medically is being at least 65 or above or permanently disabled. The VA considers us permanently disabled when we are 65. Of course, medically we meet the lowest tier.

If we stop driving because of our condition, our disability, then there's a higher tier called housebound benefit and when we get to the higher tier, the VA will pay us a little bit more money, so it's good to go up in the tiers. Then the highest tier is Aid and Attendance. That's where, on the medical side, we have to show that the person needs assistance with at least two activities of daily living, which includes bathing, dressing, toileting, eating, and transferring. If the person needs two of those five, then they can get that highest tier — Aid and Attendance.

In order to be eligible after we meet the medical and the military criteria, we also have to meet the financial criteria and so we have to be under certain income limits and we also have to be under certain asset limits.

Once we qualify the VA will actually pay the veteran or the widow directly a check through automatic deposit every single month the amount that they have been awarded based on what their income is minus medical expenses, up to the monthly maximum.

For example, currently the monthly maximum for the veteran with no dependents is $1,072 per month. For the widow, it's $1,404, and that's under the base pension. (The numbers I gave you before were under the Aid and Attendance level.) That's one of the things we have to do is find out which level are you going to be and see what our potential is.

Ultimately, what they are receiving is a monthly check that's tax-free that they then can apply toward their medical care, or their private medical care.

One of the objections we get from clients sometimes is "I don't want to use VA doctors". That's okay with me. You don't have to. This is going to allow you to have the money to pay to whoever your medical providers are.

There is a Veteran's long-term care facility not far where Linda's parents live, but I know they don't have to stay there to receive the VA benefit. I asked Victoria to further explain these types of benefits regarding assisting living and memory care communities..

Those are two independent types of veteran's benefits and, in fact, many Veterans cannot stay at a VA facility because for federal VA facilities, you have to have a service-con-

*nected disability. For the improved pension for wartime
veteran, you do not have any service-connected disability.
You are disabled because of life and so you can stay in any
environment — your own home, someone else's home, in
assisted living, or in a nursing home that's private and that
you choose.*

As I brought up earlier, Linda was aware of this benefit
for her parents, and had sent in an application, but hasn't
heard back for over a year. They weren't receiving any
care at home or at an assisted living community at the
time of application. Victoria continued:

*We do have to show that they are disabled at the time of
application. If we are seeking Aid and Attendance, the
highest level, then yes we have to have verification from the
doctor stating that they need that level of care and then we
have to show that someone is providing that level of care.
Why some people don't get approved, it's not because they
don't meet the level of care need. It's because if they're not
paying for care then they have access income and so we've
got to be paying for the care to reduce our income so that we
meet the income standard.*

*Under the aid and Attendance on level of care, the
maximum for a veteran is $1,788 per month, which is just
over the $21,000 per year. For a veteran who has a depen-
dent– and usually that is a spouse — it's $2,120 per month*

and then the widow is $1,149 per month. Those are the maximums currently. If you've got medical care of $10,000 a month, the VA is not going to pay you $10,000 — they will still limit it to their maximum monthly.

If your care is the exact same amount as your income, so your income is resulting at zero after you're paying for your care, then you will get this maximum. Again, for the veteran who has no dependent that's currently $1,788 a month. A veteran with one dependent is currently $2,120, and the widow or a widow is currently $1,149 per month. Those numbers are adjusted annually. If Social Security increases the COLA (Cost of Living), the VA's COLA increases the exact same percentage each year.

As far as asset qualification, the applicant's assets have to be at under a certain limit and the veteran's benefit manual lists that limit currently as $80,000. The VA also can consider the applicant's age when considering whether or not they have what's called "sufficient means to pay themselves." The older a person is and the closer to death — which is what's they're presuming based on age — the less they expect him to have with regards to finances. We use $80,000 as our trigger point and then if the person is elderly, like 85 or older, we may want to reduce the assets even well below 80.

How we reduce assets currently is that we can either transfer excess assets by taking the person's name off of it and putting *it into someone else's name — doing a complete transfer so that the applicant has no rights to that money anymore — or we transfer into certain types of qualifying trusts. Or sometimes they roll their money into certain types of annuities where they can still get an income stream to help offset excessive medical expenses even beyond what the Aid and Attendance will help us pay for. Those are the three primary methods: transfer to a person, transfer to a trust, or purchase an annuity.*

Under the current law, there is no prohibition against that. What this does is really help your traditional middle-class hardworking individuals who save enough to have a comfortable living while everything is going well with no crisis but they don't have enough to really offset an extended period of care. When they run out of money, their only option may be to go into a nursing home and qualify for Medicaid and get base-level care.

What the VA benefit does is try to delay the need to go to a nursing home and get on Medicaid, which is another federal benefit program, and allow the person to stretch out their money because they're getting assistance from the VA to stay in an environment that is more supportive of their independent living. I don't mean they're independent individuals. What I mean is they are in a less restrictive environment, which is what our social policy calls for in the United States.

That's what this benefit does. Helping people plan to preserve their resources with the aid of the VA benefit then helps maintain quality of life. That's what our firm does to make sure that person doesn't have to sacrifice quality of life because they are aging or disabled or both.

There are different ways to do it right. Out approval rate in my office is, on average, 44 days, which is well below what I think is the national average which is, for veterans, about six to nine months; for widows it can be longer because they're lower priority to the system. When we do our applications, we're not just filling out the VA forms that they require, but we substantiate everything we put into the forms. We are actually including all income verification, the statement from Social Security, the statement from their pensions.

We're including all bank statements for the month of eligibility. That way, the VA doesn't have to question anything. It's there. Whereas, other organizations and certain veteran service organizations, will fill out all the right VA forms, but then they don't submit anything to verify; those applications take longer.

The VA forms are available on the VA website, but there's more than just the application form that completes a package. It's about having all the right forms and also acknowledging that the VA updates them. They are in the process of updating all their forms right now and once they update one, you cannot use an old form. When you go to a veteran service organization, make sure that the organization representative didn't just pull out a copied form from their drawer that might have been in that drawer for the last six months or a year. You need to make sure that you are getting the most updated forms from the website.

Linda was surprised and thrilled to hear about different programs for her parents that she'd had little or no knowledge about, including benefits through Medicare and Medicaid, the possibility of receiving money for her father's life insurance policy, and the financial assistance available through the VA for her father and her mother. She has quite a bit of information to share with her father and her siblings on the next call.

* * *

CHAPTER THREE

Getting Professional Advice

Many family caregivers attempt to try to do things alone for a while and make decisions alone regarding their parents, spouse, or other loved ones. Not long ago, Linda's mother had a fall and was taken to the hospital. Fortunately, she was going to be fine, but she had to go into skilled nursing for rehabilitation. Because Linda had not yet learned of the resources available to her, she had an unpleasant experience that added to her stress, as well as to her parents' stress.

I shared with Linda that there are many professional resources available to provide advice and help in navigating through the process of caring for someone. I asked Linda to join me on a call with some professionals in the industry regarding geriatric consulting and elder law. Because of my own experience in the area of senior placement, I provided her with additional insights as well.

GERIATRIC CONSULTING AND ELDERCARE MANAGEMENT

Sometimes families need an advisor and seniors need an advocate to help with the myriad options and information to be aware of. Put simply, as people age, families are often faced with issues and decisions that can sound like a foreign language. Or they realize that a loved one has needs and they have no idea where to go to find resources for those needs.

Marcy Baskin, an eldercare manager for Senior Care Authority, explained to Linda the role of geriatric consulting and more specifically, the role of an eldercare manager.

An Eldercare Manager should be able do the following three things:

- *Identify the family's priorities, both immediate and long term*

- *Recognize any barriers to getting the care or services needed*

- *Have a working knowledge of services and providers that may be of help*

This may sound simple, but each of those steps involves many, many smaller steps. Families are often caught off guard, especially in a crisis situation, which unfortunately is when most people call me. No one likes to speculate, when things are going well, about what will happen if mom gets dementia, dad breaks a hip and ends up in the hospital, all of a sudden a loved one who has not been seen for awhile is repeating herself and seems confused or agitated for no reason.

Identifying priorities covers a very large territory. If the family is in crisis (medical, unsafe living situation, etc.), we look at how to take things out of crisis mode. For example, if mom has been hospitalized for a medical condition and during her stay, we start to see behaviors that indicate short term memory loss or other signs of dementia, we have to think about what that means when she is released. Where will she go? Rehab? Home with caregivers? To assisted living or other residential care? We take a realistic look at what will serve the individual best — and that's a big conversation right there.

Then there are barriers, such as emotional stress about wanting to go home and not be "placed." And if going home means having home care, who figures out what is needed, how much care will be required, whether there are modifications to the home that need to be made for safety and comfort?

A big issue is money. Getting old and needing care is not an inexpensive proposition. It's lovely to have healthy financial resources but, no matter what, a detailed financial picture needs to be drawn to know what the options are. Is there long-term care insurance? Veteran's benefits eligibility? Life Insurance? If long-term care is what we are looking at, does a house need to be sold to pay for that? What about a reverse mortgage? How do we know if that's a good idea or not? Can family members contribute to care costs? Are there powers of attorney in place? Advance directives? A POLST on file?

And if that isn't enough, there is the entirely separate category of family dynamics and how that plays into the big picture. So you can see how this can be a lot of pressure on a family, arriving at their doorstep all at once.

Visiting with the family is an important part of the process, along with encouraging them to ask me a lot of questions. Once they become a client, I become a partner in the process for as little or as much as they would like to use my services. I have accompanied someone to medical appointments, ensured that their pets are not overlooked, found home-care, located residential care options, helped implement a discharge plan, helped get referrals for providers, etc. The whole gamut.

What I try to do is break everything down into baby steps, see who can do what, and track that each step is implemented to make way for the next. I like to share that I know firsthand what families are going through. As I always say, I went to boot camp when each of my parents became ill — Dad with multiple physical disorders, starting in his late 60s, and my Mom with Alzheimer's Disease. Particularly with my mother, I had absolutely no idea where to start, who to talk to, or how to know what was best for her.

My experience was that even in my 50s, with all the life experience I'd already had, all the cars, appliances, homes I had bought, I was completely unprepared to shop for care options and find resources to help my parents. I did it, eventually, but it was frustrating, overwhelming, and very isolating. Not a good place to be when I was already dealing with the loss of my parents as I knew them.

The other part was that it felt like I had no one to talk to about it as I was caregiving or as I was overseeing care decisions for someone else. That's an experience like no other. An eldercare manager can't change what life has thrown at a family, but she can definitely take the edge off some of those moments where the path is very unclear.

Though it is quite clear that often the elderly would like to live at home for the rest of their lives, many cannot live safely at home. There are numerous reasons for this:

- *Alzheimer's or another form of dementia which is becoming too difficult or unsafe for the family to provide care.*

- *Family dynamics, including those living long distances from one another.*

- *There is no family to take care of the senior.*

- *High cost of outside caregivers when assistance is needed regularly.*

SENIOR PLACEMENT ADVISORS

After Linda's mother was discharged from the skilled nursing facility, a good option may have been for her to take one more step before going home, assuming she was able to go home. She may have been able to go to an assisted living location, maybe even one with as few as five or six other residents, where the caregiver-to-resident ratio is excellent for someone in her particular situation.

With over 45,000 licensed assisted living locations in the United States and only 15,000 skilled nursing facilities, there's movement toward long-term living at various types of assisted living locations. These can range from smaller four-person residential care homes to larger, 200-bed assisted living communities.

Today, skilled nursing facilities are placing greater emphasis on short-term stays over long-term stays. Short-term rehabilitation has become a necessity for skilled nursing facilities, bringing in additional revenue and higher margins.

Because of this shift in long-term care living, companies of all types and sizes are starting up to capture a segment of this growing population. One type of company is known as a senior placement agency. This segment of our industry has the ability to provide tremendous value to families whose loved ones need a different place to live and be cared for. I provided Linda with an explanation of this type of service. I also wanted her to be aware of similar services that are not offering the quality assistance I believe is needed for families.

Full-Service, Senior Placement Agencies have local representation that are trained and experienced to assist with various aspects of the placement process, whether they be with assisted living communities, memory care locations, or residential care homes. Commissions are normally paid by the particular locations to the agency (similar to the real estate model), so families may not have to pay additional fees. These companies usually represent most of the locations in the area. Services may include assessing the needs of the family's loved one, meeting "face to face" with the family, providing background information on locations including any state reports noting citations or deficiencies, accompanying families on visits, being familiar with each location, helping negotiate the best rates and assisting with any medical information from physicians and other resources to help with a smooth transition. Though some of these agencies have an online presence where some information can be learned about the senior, the goal is to meet locally with the family and guide them to the best options. The key benefit of this service is having a non-biased professional who assists the family through a process that can be a daunting task filled with stress.

Referral Services — As the name describes, a "referral" is when someone is directed to a source for help or information. Though this is not a service I would recommend, there are scenarios that you can find yourself in without even realizing it:

- You may fill out a form online about a particular assisted living community or care home where they ask a few questions on a web form. In some cases, they automatically send information directly to several assisted living facilities and have them contact the family directly. The challenge is that the "referral" is sent to many locations, sometimes a dozen or more, and representatives from the locations will call the family contact by phone. The companies do not have local representation to meet with the families. If a representative from the "referral agency" does call you on the phone (usually from a call center), they have not usually even seen the locations they are referring the family to. Also, the myriad phone calls often adds additional stress to the situation.

- WHAT TO DO? If you search online for information, make sure you read the fine print so they are not automatically sending your information to several facilities. Also, if you receive a call from a representative of the referral agency, tell them you do not want to receive any phone calls from the various assisted living locations and not to share your information with any of these locations.

- Upon being discharged from a hospital or skilled nursing facility, they may provide a list of assisted living locations to the family in the area. These locations are just a list and have not been visited or reviewed by the hospital or nursing facility. These locations may also have multiple citations issued against them that the hospital or nursing facility is unaware of. The families will also have to visit and determine on their own if the location is the right fit for their loved one, which can be time consuming and stressful, especially if your loved one is being discharged in a matter of a few days.

- WHAT TO DO? Ask the discharge planner, social worker, or other representative if they know of a "full-service" senior placement agency, as described previously.

As in Linda's case, helping to reduce family stress and not add to it during this decision making process is essential as the need continues to rise for advice on assisting living options.

ELDER LAW ATTORNEY

Elder Law is a generic term used in this field. You may think all elder law attorneys do the same thing, but there are different specializations in this particular field. I advised Linda that she would need the services of an elder law attorney in regards to legal documents that should be implemented and expectations in regards to long-term care, such as nursing. I asked Phillip Lindsley, a certified Elder Law attorney and the founder of San Diego Elder Law Center, to explain more details of this profession and the areas that could be of help to Linda.

When I first started practicing, in 1980, they did not have the field of elder law. That didn't come about until some years later. We had different labels for those of us who did estate planning, that had an emphasis on incapacity and disability issues, mental health issues, and the like. Those who were interested in that area tended to also be concerned about community resources, public benefits programs, and, in the case of elders, Medicare rules and regulations. With time, come the late 80s, you first started hearing the term "elder law," and then slowly we started identifying ourselves as elder law attorneys, which now has come to mean a pretty defined set of legal skills.

The National Elder Law Foundation is the accrediting organization, and they have some definitions of the various skills that are part of an elder law practitioner. The core of the field of elder law really is the familiarity with rules and regulations regarding public benefits, Medicaid, Medicare, VA benefits, and community resources. In addition, a good elder law practitioner should understand the laws concerning incapacity and disability, and be able to put that together, understanding the resources and understanding the challenges of incapacity and disability for the clients and their families.

Elder abuse at facilities is a different beast. For that, you'll need a litigation attorney. Some of them identify themselves as elder law practitioners, but that's more of a marketing thing. Most elder law practitioners — and the field of elder law — are more about planning. That's different than filing lawsuit for injuries, but certainly an elder law attorney should be willing to and to address grievances, if that's what it takes.

Some firms, like ours, have a full time social worker on staff, just to help be able to go to facilities and talk out our issues and negotiate better treatment for our clients if that's an issue, so we don't have to be filing actions. If necessary, we do, though, and I think if you're looking for an elder law practitioner, you should look for somebody who can do those type of things as well as look at the estate plans and make sure that they have the proper language.

WHAT NURSING HOMES DON'T ALWAYS TELL YOU

After Linda's mother had her fall, she was taken to the hospital, then to a skilled nursing facility, then she was discharged to her home, where her father needed to provide care and supervision. Her father was not equipped to provide her with this assistance, but the family didn't think they had a choice in this matter.

Quite often, family members whose loved one is going to be discharged from a skilled nursing facility may not be ready for them to go home yet. Usually when that happens, everybody is in a panic. The reason they are in a panic is because the decision is often made a day or two prior to discharge that particular senior or family member, and everybody is scrambling to either get family assistance, find in-home care or assisted living.

I asked Phil to provide his input to this type of situation so Linda's family does not have this negative experience again.

Well, first off, in most of the scenarios of someone being discharged, the families welcome the discharge. I certainly wouldn't want to be in a skilled nursing facility any longer than I needed to be. There are situations where, as you said, they just don't seem quite ready yet. Like Linda's situations, sometimes the family can't visualize any level of care anymore as appropriate as skilled nursing. The problem is the incentives for the family and facility may not always align. For the family, they want the best setting for the level of care that is appropriate, and for the facility, their business is they want as good a profit margin as they can get. The fact of the matter is, they can get a better profit margin treating people for the short term, when Medicare or private insurance is paying, and less so for longer term, which is sometimes known as custodial patients. They have an incentive to move people out as quickly as possible, and that may not always be identical to what is medically the best option. That's where the struggle begins.

People have rights at that point that they're simply not aware of, both under federal and state law. The problem is the facilities usually are delivering the information in commandments, rather than conversation. As you pointed out, they say something like, "we're discharging your father

Thursday at 10 a.m. Have the car ready, and I'll help you load him in the back." That doesn't sound like there's a whole lot of room for discussion of options of whether or not that's appropriate. Most people assume that's what they have to do, whether or not that seems prudent to them or not.

Families do have rights, and you should note that most of the law in this area is federal. States may add to those, but they can't do less. They can add more. We have some extra laws out here in California, but most of what I'm talking about here is federal law and applies everywhere. Most discharges are considered voluntary, the vast majority of them. When they say, "It's time to go on Thursday," and you don't know you have options and leave, that's considered a voluntary discharge. It may not have sounded like it to you, but it is. If you are willing, however, to say, "No, I don't think he is ready. Let's talk about this," then a new process that people aren't aware of comes into play. It's considered involuntary discharge.

There are only six reasons, under federal law, that they can discharge people who are willing to say, "Now wait a minute here, I'm not so sure this is appropriate." One, is if they can prove it's necessary for their welfare and their needs can't be met by the facility. Another one is because their health has improved or they no longer need that level of care. Another is the safety of individuals in the facility is endangered. The fourth is that the health of other people is endangered. Five is that there is refusal after proper notice, and legal process to pay. The final one is the facility ceases to exist.

Notably, what's not on that list, is, "We don't have any custodial beds." This is something people often hear. Or, "We are a short term care facility only." This is where that incentive for the facility to not have people who are going to be on Medicaid, comes into play. Under the law, those are not grounds for discharge. That is quite clear. Form of payment is irrelevant. You cannot discharge, and there is no such thing as not having a "custodial bed". If you are in a bed, you've got a bed. If Medicare isn't paying anymore, that may be a correct statement. It's not grounds for discharge. Conversion to Medicaid is not grounds for discharge. Difficult, demanding problem residents aren't grounds for discharge. Somebody who talks a lot or wanders around the facility, or howls at night, these are challenges for them. These people need to be somewhere. Those are not grounds for discharge.

Even it you are being told Medicare won't pay anymore, that doesn't necessarily make it so. It may be true. That's a whole issue in itself. Facilities are often applying the wrong standard about whether or not Medicare pays or not, and not even bothering to bill Medicare. It is an issue the family needs to address. Number one, they need to ask, "Is this true? Is Medicare no longer paying? Do we have any appeal *rights with Medicare on that issue?" The answer to that is always "yes." If Medicare is no longer paying, then the family has the right to discuss whether or not mom needs to stay there, private pay, or if the family is able to qualify for the assistance from the long-term Medicaid program. That particular Medicaid program has some substantial middle-class benefits. A lot of people will qualify for assistance under the program that are not aware of that fact. If somebody wants to stay there and do an application for that program, and thinks they may be eligible for assistance, that is not grounds for discharge. Again, Medicare isn't paying anymore, may or may not be a correct statement. It's not grounds for discharge. It's grounds for the family to discuss whether or not there are other program options out there other than Medicare.*

If Medicare truly has stopped coverage, the family can always private pay if they cannot qualify for Medicaid. Of course, again, make sure the statement that Medicare is not paying anymore is a correct statement. There's been a lot of litigation on that. There have been interesting changes of the regulations in the last few years, potentially extending Medicare coverage in skilled care. That said, let's assume that in fact Medicare payment no longer is an option, yes, they certainly have the right to stay if they are private pay, and they certainly should take a look and see if there is a possibility for assistance under the Medicaid program. Again, a lot of families have no idea about the benefits that can come there. There are particularly liberal eligibility rules if there is a spouse, what we call spousal protection rules, that allow quite a bit for assets and still qualify for the program. I would suggest anybody who finds themselves in that situation, and they don't think discharge back home, or to assisted living, or board and care, is appropriate, consult with an elder law attorney who is knowledgeable about Medicaid in their area. They may be pleasantly surprised.

People have a right to written notification about discharge. Theoretically, the grounds for discharge are supposed to be adequately documented in the chart. The law requires that there be an exploration by the discharge planners as to the alternative in the community. The law mandates that the family be involved with this discussion, if there is a family that wants to be involved. There's got to be sufficient orientation and preparation that the facility must provide and a post-discharge plan of care developed in consultation with the family.

For best results, it takes somebody, even themselves, to be willing to be an advocate and ask questions, or a family member being willing to step up and say, "Well, wait a minute here. I've got some questions." Or, "How's that going to work?"

I often tell my clients that if every time they are told something at a facility that sounds like a commandment or a statement about what is going to be, that they get in the habit in their mind, of adding to the front of the statement this sentence: "We would like to talk to you about..." Or "What is your opinion about...?" Just by doing that, you'll have a much better idea of what the law requires. That is what the law requires. The law requires a discussion with you, a thoughtful discussion, and an actual written plan by them that makes sense.

The skilled nursing facility may be correct to say they've done all they can do. However, in Linda's mother's case, the doctor said, "Listen, we are going to discharge your mom, but she is going to need 24-care, or somebody with her all the time to decrease the chance of a fall," or whatever the case may be. That really is what was really challenging for Linda's family. They didn't know that. "Wait, we work. My father can't handle it, and I don't have anybody to come in. How much is that going to be?" This is a big issue. Phil responded:

Yes, on one hand, you have the clinical opinion. On the other hand, you have the practical considerations of support network and the cost. One family may have a large number of active involved people, and with some community support, a little extra for some paid caregivers, dad may be able to stay home. Another family may not have the same resources, and there's just no financial way given their income and assets that they are going to be able to pay for 24/7 caregivers. If that's the case, maybe the discharge is inappropriate. You can't discuss discharges in a vacuum.

It may make sense for one person to leave skilled nursing because they have options for lower levels of placement that make sense clinically and make sense financially, whether it's at home or assisted living or memory care. It may make sense. If it is not an option, and for that family it does not make sense, either because of the level of care required and the family resources, or the finances, the discharge is not appropriate. Maybe the family member is exactly where they need to be, regardless of what the facility feels about their profit margin, should that person start getting assistance from Medicaid and stay there.

I urge people to get involved here and know what their rights are... and if things aren't going well, whether it is a care concern or a discharge issue, don't start yelling at the nursing assistant. I know you're frustrated. I know you want to see the best care for your parent. You're yelling at the wrong person. Yelling isn't going to get you what you want. More likely that not, I think people who get overly frustrated end up with restraining orders. Then the best family advocate is sidelined.

What you need to do is talk to those people calmly. What you need to do is talk to the Director of Nursing, or somebody higher up. Say, "I have these issues. What do you think about this? What are you going to do?" That will be a much better conversation. If you hear things in that conversation you like, such as, "I agree. We need to check your father's incontinence issue more frequently." Or "We need to turn him more frequently." Then you go home and you write a letter to that person and say, "I was so happy to speak to you today. I am happy that you say you are going to do this, this, and this." Once you put something in writing and send it to the facility, you have elevated yourself as to a person that will hold them accountable. They have to put that letter in the file. Now there is something objective. Don't yell at the nursing assistant. Talk to the people higher up, and document, document, document. Don't be hesitant to find out what your appeal rights are in your county. You will, under federal and state law, have the right to file complaints and appeal. That documentation can only help.

ESTATE PLANNING

Many make plans ahead of time to prepare for when someone dies. However, there is planning that should be done while someone is still alive. Sometimes this type of planning is overlooked by families, which can make things very difficult when important decisions have to be made. I asked Jamie Watson, from the law firm of Gaw Van Male, to go over with Linda the importance of estate planning and to discuss the planning documents her family should have so they do not create unnecessary stress and possible legal issues later.

When folks come see me and ask about doing estate planning, really what I try to explain to them putting together an estate plan encompasses multiple things and we'll talk about that. An estate plan is a system of lifetime management of the assets in the event that, for example, if I've become incapacitated, who do I want to manage those assets, how do I want those assets managed, who has the power to sell assets, who has the power to buy assets. Really, what I think most people understand is a designation of your wishes when you pass away. How do I want those assets to go my loved ones or my children, my spouse, and under what terms do I want those assets to pass to those individuals?

For most people, (95% of my clients who walk in here), we talk about a living trust. Really, that's the centerpiece of an estate plan. A lot folks know and have heard the term "revocable living trust" or" living trust" and, really, that's the hub of most people's estate planning documents. The living trust is the designation of the wishes, how assets are to be managed during my lifetime and also where those assets pass upon my death. Surrounding the living trust, if that's a centerpiece, are several other key documents. To me, one of the most critical is a durable power of attorney for finance. We'll get into that a little bit. That's a designation of the assets, outside of the trust.

For example, my home goes inside of the trust, physically moving the title into the trust. My bank accounts physically move inside of the trust. Well, certain assets like IRAs, 401(k)s, 403(b)s, you don't physically put inside of a trust. What you need in that circumstance is a well-drafted power of attorney to be able to deal with those assets in the event that I'm unable to or I'm out of the country, I'm incapacitated or I'm just not able to deal with those assets outside of trust.

Certainly a really important document is also an advance health care directive, designation of wishes in the event that I can't make medical decisions for myself. That's another component of the estate plan.

For most, their main asset is their primary residence. You can have a great trust and it can be the best-drafted trust in the world, but if you don't fund the trust, meaning move the assets into the trust, it doesn't do anything for you.

What I find is a lot of folks come in and have done a living trust, but when they go to refinance their house, the bank says, "Well, you need to take the house out of the trust so we can refinance it," and they never put the house back into the trust. It can create a lot of issues and the folks thought they've avoided probate maybe on the death of one of their spouses or the death of the second individual, married couple, and they come to realize that the house was taken out of the trust and it was never put back in. You have deeds that are a component of the estate plan.

Also, a lot of times, we do Health and Privacy Act releases, so designated individuals can have access to medical records, which is extremely important when they're dealing with medical situations, especially aging clients. Also, coordination of beneficiary designations outside of the trust, so 401(k)s, 403(b)s, IRAs, making sure how assets pass to your loved ones are coordinated with the terms of the trust. Often times, we coordinate the beneficiary designations with the trust as well.

I brought up to Jamie that Linda's parents never did a trust, but there is a will. It says where everything should go and who's going to get jewelry and other things. I asked Jamie to help Linda understand better the benefits to a trust.

Most folks, what they don't realize, when we talk about a will and when it is effective. A will, in the term that folks and the legal community use, "speaks death," meaning that the provisions of that will only become effective the moment I pass away. Often times, for individuals, you're looking for assistance, especially. I've seen many, many clients who have loved ones who are starting to decline mentally with the onset of maybe dementia. It's becoming more and more frequent that I see clients like that. Often, a will is not going to dictate the management of those assets during my lifetime. It only talks about what happens to those assets at death. The trust is a system management for assets during your lifetime if you're starting to decline mentally and you're unable to manage your assets.

The other major reason people use a trust over a will is the avoidance of probate. When I have a will and it speaks of death, like I said, you have to submit that will to the probate court, which is a public proceeding. A lot of folks like the privacy of the living trust. They don't want their assets in the public eye, and having probate is public. A lot of folks, when they submit the will to probate, don't realize that that's a long process, six months, a year-long process depending on where you're located throughout the United States and on the courts.

Whereas with the living trust, you don't need to go to probate. You can come into the attorney's office who drafted it and they can administer the trust in the office in a private setting. Most folks like the privacy aspect of the living trust as opposed to a will and a lot of folks like the efficiency of the trust administration a lot more.

Though I mentioned to Linda earlier about getting a power of attorney, she hadn't done it yet. Now that her mother has fallen and she's seeing firsthand more of the issues that can arise and complicate things, I wanted to emphasize the importance of getting this done. Jamie offered Linda advice about this document and how estate planning and power of attorney relate to each other.

To me, the power of attorney, if you do nothing else, especially if you're an aging individual, is just such an important document to have, regardless of whether or not you do the revocable living trust. The reason is that if you do not have a power of attorney and you start to lose your capacity and you have an inability to make financial decisions, the only alternative that your loved ones have is often going to a conservatorship, which is incredibly expensive, in terms of legal fees. It can be a very demeaning process, because you, as an individual now, are dragged in front of the court and your loved ones are asking the court to enter an order against you that you don't have the ability to manage your assets and you don't have the capacity to manage your assets.

Having a well-drafted power of attorney is an extremely critical thing. I tell my clients, "Look, if you do nothing else, if you walk out of here and do nothing else, just do yourself a favor and get a well-drafted power of attorney, because it'll enable you do to so many other things in the future."

Now, that being said, you alluded to the fact that it scares people. Well, it should scare people a little bit because you are giving the agent a lot of authority. My thought is that's why you carefully select that individual. You make sure that it's someone that's close to you, that you can count on to make critical decisions for you at critical times. A lot of care and a lot of thought needs to go into that decision.

There are generally two types of powers of attorney. This is specifically related to financial powers of attorney. I kind of touched on powers of attorney for health care, but specifically in relation to financial powers of attorney, there are really two types. One is called an "immediately effective power of attorney," meaning when I sign the document and I name you, you now have the authority to have total capacity the moment I sign that. You have the ability now to go out and take action under that power of attorney. Sometimes, that scares individuals, but I'll explain my bias and why I like immediately effective power of attorney.

The other type of power of attorney is what's called a "springing power of attorney." Think of it as springing into effect only when a doctor — or normally two doctors — declare that I'm incapacitated. It's effective only at the time that I don't have the ability to act for myself, according to two doctors, or whatever the instrument says.

To review, there are generally two types of powers of attorney. One, as we've been talking about, is the financial power of attorney. The second is, and certainly I think is a very, very critical document and most folks, I really encourage having one of these in place too, it's a financial power of attorney for health care. I can name someone as my agent under that document and they now have the ability, when I can't make my own medical decisions, to act on my behalf. Really, it deals with end of life type decisions. Do I want to be on a feeding tube? Do I want to have any artificial ventilation? What type of pain relief do I want at the end of my life? It deals with those decisions, but also lets you deal with my day-to-day medical decisions. Should I go see this doctor or should I go see that doctor? Very important document.

The other thing I'd leave you with is when you're seeking out legal advice, you don't, as the consumer, typically know the questions to ask. You should have an attorney or another professional for that matter who you feel comfortable with and asking questions that you necessarily haven't even thought of. You really want to have someone who's listening and asking and extracting questions and trying to get thoughtful answers out of you as opposed to someone who just produces the document.

* * *

Linda will now make sure she retains the services of a eldercare consultant and uses the services of a full-service placement agency. She is now clear about not having to go through this alone.

Also, she now has the power of attorney forms completed and she and her father are working with an attorney to put together her parents' estate plan.

She is also much clearer as to the best way to deal with hospitals and skilled nursing facilities, especially if the family member is not ready to be discharged.

CHAPTER FOUR
The Realities of Long-Term Care

Long-term care can mean many different things to various people. I like to think of it as long-term living versus long-term care. There are numerous options for Linda and her parents to choose from. For example, if they stay at home, they can consider getting a home care agency. Or what about hiring a caregiver — will that be less expensive? Also, if they stay at home, going to an adult day care program could be an option. What are the cost differences between assisted living and home care? How does assisted living compare to skilled nursing? Linda heard from various experts I arranged for her to talk with to get the answers to these questions.

There is a lot to consider, but I wanted Linda to get all the information so that she, her siblings, and their parents can make intelligent decisions together for the parents' long-term living plan. I spoke to Linda about communicating with her parents about this plan and also preparing her for the fact that guilt could set in on her part if things don't go according to plan.

TALK TO YOUR PARENTS NOW TO AVOID PROBLEMS LATER

As people age, there is a strong chance that some kind of long-term care will be needed. According to the Department of Health and Human Services, "About 70 percent of individuals over age 65 will require at least some type of long-term care services during their lifetime."

So, knowing that your parent or spouse will probably need some sort of care at home, in assisted living, or in nursing care (the lesser likelihood), it's imperative to have open conversations about the possibility:

- Is there any long-term care insurance?

- If a parent is a veteran, do you have their discharge papers and other information? (there are benefits from the VA for a veteran or surviving spouse).

- Is there life insurance? (some life insurance policies can be converted for long-term care assistance).

- Regardless of the type of assistance needed, know what is affordable, since most long-term options are paid for privately and could end up being thousands of dollars each month.

I know what you're thinking: "My parents aren't going anywhere. They said they're just going to stay home."

That is the case with practically all seniors, but that may not be reality. Be careful what you promise before your know all the facts. Below are a couple of examples of comments I've heard from clients and their parents. They are all too common:

- "I promised my wife I would never put her in a convalescent home," said a caring husband about his wife with Alzheimer's who is also a fall and wander risk. But the home is not safe for someone in her condition. The husband is in poor health and all three children live out of state and have jobs and their own children to take of.

- "I gave my word to my father that he would not go to a nursing home, and if needed, I would make sure he gets the proper care at his home. He has lived in this home for the last 50 years." But because of the father's condition, he cannot be left alone, so in order to live at home, he needs 24-hour assistance, seven days per week. Due to the significant cost for this, the father's money will be depleted in less than one year.

There are two misconceptions that many have regarding long-term care:

- **"If I don't stay home, I'll need to go to a Nursing Home"** — There was a time when nursing homes were the main type of facility for long-term care. Many of us remember going to visit loves ones at these locations with horrible smells and less than adequate care. Today, nursing homes are mainly set up for short-term stays after being hospitalized for recovery and strengthening. Those who need to be in nursing homes for long-term care are either on Medicaid (Medi-Cal in California) or need medical care (i.e., IVs, feeding tubes, wound care, coma care, quadriplegics). Most people still believe that if they are not taken care of at their own home, they will have to go to a nursing or convalescent home. That is simply not true.

- **"Assisted Living is another name for a nursing home"** — Nursing homes are an exception rather than the rule. Many more seniors who need assistance reside in assisted living versus skilled nursing. Assisted living options range from small, family-like residential care homes to larger, full-service communities with hundreds of residents. The smaller locations are similar to living in someone's home with live-in caregivers who provide assistance. The larger locations (communities) are more like senior apartments with caregivers providing 24/7 assistance. Most that have cognitive issues like dementia also reside in these types of environments versus a nursing home.

Talk to your parents — that's essential — but be careful of the promises you make until you know all the facts.

ENSURING BEST OUTCOMES IN LONG-TERM CARE

Though we hear of horror stories in long-term care facilities, such as nursing and assisted living, as well as concern about elder abuse, there are ways to help ensure positive results from these experiences.

I was able to set up a conference call with Linda for us to speak to Sanford Horowitz, a plaintiff's attorney for over 20 years who concentrated almost all of his practice on elder abuse and neglect litigation, select medical malpractice, personal injury, though he also deals with other cases. I wanted to make sure that Linda's expectations were set correctly if she started looking at long-term care options for her parents.

I asked Sanford to talk about when someone is considering a long-term care facility, whether it is nursing or assisted living or a smaller care home, what's the best way to help ensure good outcomes?

Well, certainly one of the most important things is how you look out for your loved one, and I've done this professionally for years. I went through ten years of Alzheimer's with my own dad and it really gave me a lot of insight into how difficult this all is, because I was armed with all of this knowledge, and I still had to make sure the right things were going on. It really gave me a lot of insight into what clients go through, and the level of stress and worry.

This is going to be more and more important, so the more information people have on this complex subject, the better.

I believe strongly that families need to understand how they should interact with long-term care ownership and staff in order to ensure the best outcomes for their loved ones. And that's exactly what we all want to do is ensure the best outcomes.

Most people do a little research before they place their loves ones, but a lot of times, there's that situation when no one was thinking that way — there's a stroke, and the person goes to the hospital. Then they immediately have to go somewhere, and you didn't even get a chance to do the research.

So, obviously, the more research you could do in advance, the better. But even if it's a last minute issue, the comments I'll make here still apply. Essentially, wherever your loved one ends up, the first thing you want to do after you've met with the admissions person and they've given you the tour which of course is their best face. So, I'm going to start at the top of the food chain, the big nursing homes, but this really applies to any facility and becomes easier the smaller they are.

You want to immediately find out where the buck stops, who's in charge. And in the bigger places, there's always an administrator, and that's the person who has the most responsibility in the facility. They're usually not a health care professional, usually more of a business person, sometimes they are even a nurse as well. They sit in an office, mostly they're not out in the halls or visiting residents or your loved ones as much, although the good ones do get to know people.

So, you want to sit in that office, and you want to talk to that person, and you want to eyeball them, and you want to let them know how you're looking out for your loved one, and you want to know who they are and understand what their philosophy is, how long they've been there. These things really matter, because if that position keeps turning over, that's a red flag for you. Like any situation, if important people keep leaving, then something is not going well at the place.

You really want to get to know them, you want to do it in a way that you're not interrogating them. You want to make it friendly. I think they really are helpful. Let them know you appreciate that it's a difficult job, because it is. Let them know you do understand that. And let them know that you understand that they're caught between wanting to give the best care and overseeing people, and having personal relationships with the corporate pressures of what's usually the home office — somewhere else; it might be in a whole other state that they're sending numbers to every day about how many people are in the facility, and how much money is going in and out, and all those business things. You really want to reach them as, "My loved one is a person, and I'm a person, you're a person," and we all want this to really go the best in a humane way.

It's really good to talk to them and let them know you're really paying attention. Ask them questions about the staff. Do they give the staff insurance? Do they give them bene-fits? What's their turnover like? What kind of training do they do?

They'll appreciate that your loved one is someone to whom they're going to have to make sure they're paying atten-tion. And I hate to put it that way, because it's between your loved one and others, and a lot of people don't have anybody advocating for them. You really have to advocate and your person will get more attention that way, there's no doubt about it.

With Linda on the phone, she brought up to Sanford that it's very possible that both her parents may end up needing care. The main concern is costs. Having learned about Medicaid, she is considering just getting her parents approved on Medicaid through some effective planning by an attorney. Then, they can go into skilled nursing and have it paid for. On the other hand, she really doesn't want them to be in that environment, and they probably don't need to be. She would rather have them in a nicer assisted living environment, but it seems expensive. She wanted to know his thoughts.

The only thing I could say about expense, which is heartbreaking, since I've seen every situation, every socioeconomic, every type of family culturally is that all you could do is spend as much as you can afford, obviously.

So, if you're on Medicaid at a nursing home, you're not going to get the same kind of treatment as if you're in private pay in a small assisted living situation. But all these things still apply. All you're trying to do is the best you can with the situation you're in. No matter what the situation is, you can meet these people.

Similarly, I talked about the administrator. Then you have the person called Director of Nursing in the bigger place, and that's the person who really directs the nursing staff and the certified nursing aides or the aides in smaller places, and they're the people who are really doing the caring. So, you care about how they're being managed and how long they've been there, and how they've been treated. It filters all the way down.

I'm always surprised because people are under so much stress caring for their loved ones and trying to max out their visits, how rarely people even know the names of some of the caregivers. So, I encourage everybody to take a moment and talk to them as people. Show a little interest in them: "Oh, where are you from, and how did you choose this kind of work?" And "I really appreciate that you do this kind of work. I know it's hard."

I don't say all this to sugar coat it, I really mean this. People who generally go into these jobs have a caring heart, because they're getting paid very little. They could be, you know, flipping burgers or they could be doing retail.

They really do have a caring heart and a lot of them came to it having cared for one of their loved ones, a grandfather or a grandmother. And then they get a little jaded because they realize they can't give the care they want to give when there's not enough staff and they're not having enough training because they're just desperately trying to get through the day.

So, you really want to know who these people are and get into their core a little, the ones who are caring the most for your loved one. Get to know them a little, because it's the same as everything else in life. If you have some rapport with people, they're going to go a little further for you, it's only human nature.

And if they know a little bit more about your loved one, it's not just your demented dad, like my dad near the end, who couldn't talk as much. It's my dad who did all these things in his life that I've told them about. I've made him more of an interesting human. Then they might look for glimpses of that more often.

I can't really stress how important it is to get to know who the key people are from the top to the bottom. If you're in a situation where you're going to the dining hall, especially more in assisted living where people are doing that a lot more than they are in nursing homes, where most of the residents can't make the dining hall. Even with the kitchen staff, you want to know who everybody is and be friendly, because they all matter.

And when you're not there at three a.m., sometimes it's one of those people who fill in, even though the facility is not telling you that. Everybody you could be kind to and try to have some kindness returned really does benefit you and your loved one.

I brought up with Sanford that Linda's two siblings live out of town and are not nearly as involved as they should be. The burden is falling on Linda. I asked Sanford to discuss some of the negative situations that can occur when the family is not involved.

It's a cruel world, I always say, but there's plenty of beauty, as well. So, the sad part which hit me when I started doing this practice. Funny enough the case decided, Delaney v.

Baker, when I was a very young lawyer, we're going back to 1993, that Ms. Delaney walked in my office and it hasn't changed much since then. She was very involved with what happened and bad things still happened. Ever since then, what's been chilling for me is, you have to realize I only handle cases where the family was involved. Otherwise, they wouldn't know what happened.

They wouldn't have the wherewithal and the anger to seek justice. I can't tell you how many people sit in my office and say, "I just don't want this to happen to anybody else". The short answer to your question is no. I think that even worse things are happening to people who don't have advocates, because I'm only hearing about bad stories from people who are in there begging the nursing home to do something different, or on the tail of the assisted living owner and saying, "Look, there are not enough people here" or "You're not monitoring my loved one enough like you said you would," or "You're not turning on the alarm so they keep falling," or whatever the issue is.

I only have people show up in my office who have the story about what happened. It's a little chilling to me what must be going on for everybody else who doesn't have the advocate.

Showing up matters. It's better to show up less often for 15 minutes than just do you three-hour visit once a week. The more you show up, the more you know the people, look at *the chart a little; try to use the doctor's advocate. The more you're involved, the more you're helping to ensure your loved one will get better care.*

Linda and her siblings have to think what is best for their parents. I realize her brother, and maybe her sister, are concerned about what money will be left to them when their parent's both pass. However, I emphasized to Linda to do what's best for her parents with the time they have left and keep them safe. If she does, there will not be guilt and she'll be able to sleep better at night.

WHAT'S IN-HOME CARE ALL ABOUT?

Linda is considering the option of in-home care for her parents, at least until they move to a long-term care facility, whether nursing or assisted living.

Bob Nations is the co-founder of a Senior Helpers in-home care franchise in the area where Linda's parents live. Bob explained to Linda about this type of service.

What we do is non-medical homecare. What that means is that we go to the person's living environment, whether that's an apartment or a residential home or in some cases even in Assisted Living, or we've even been hired to work in nursing homes. We go into that environment and help them do whatever they need that is non-medical.

Non-medical is kind of a gray area because we do bathing, dressing, we do bed management; we can check blood pressures, those kinds of things. But the medical side of it is doing injections or doing physical therapy or doing speech therapy or occupational therapy. Those are all medical-oriented things we don't do. Now, we could follow directions by a licensed professional who does those medical things, but we can't do that on our own.

Our service differs from a home health agency. A home health agency can go into the same environments and do the medical side of things. And typically, what those people can handle is the medical side such as the services I just mentioned like injections. There are two types of home health agencies: Medicare and private pay.

The Medicare rule within home health is they cannot do continuous care. What they can do is go into a home environment and help somebody for a short term in that if, in the case of my grandmother, she's fallen and broken her hip. Now, she's come home and the doctor ordered physical therapy, she could in fact move back to her home now and get physical therapy done through a physical therapist in the home and do that up in to the point where she no longer needs it. And she also needs to show progress.

So, typically, Medicare would approve physical therapy in the home for about 60 days and that physical therapist comes a couple of times a week and works with an individual and gets them back up on their feet. So, that's a home health agency.

Now, home health agency would sometimes also do the private care things which means Medicare will pay for parts of it, and then you have to pay privately for the other parts of it.

The other type of agency that goes into people's homes that we work a lot with is the hospice organization. That's when it's been determined that their life is shorter and they may be in a position where they're going to start experiencing pain and discomfort. A family would bring it up, having a hospice agency to help manage the pain, and manage the last months or years of a person's life.

We know that people, as we age, are likely to get at least pre-chronic problems; arthritis being number one. So, that leads to a spot where people aren't going to keep the same lifestyle or the same things that they've been doing in the past.

And I'm just going to use arthritis as an example because it's the number one chronic illness in our country. Because I have arthritis, I may not be keeping my house up to the same level as I always have. So, in that case it could very well be having someone from in home care come in and help do the housework, a service that a non-medical home care agency might do. But also because of my arthritis, I'm not cooking, and I'm not eating as well as I used to. Well, that starts the vicious cycle. You start spiraling down because when you stop eating as well as you always have then, in fact, your health starts deteriorating.

So, the best thing to do is for people to start at when they start noticing signs that "I'm not eating as well, I'm not eating as often, and I'm not keeping my house up."

When you start seeing signs like that, particularly family emergencies, for example you are visiting mom and she kept an immaculate house. All of a sudden she's not doing that, and when you look in the refrigerator there's no real food in there, those are signs that, "Oh you know, she may need some help." Because what's happening today is most of the time people don't call for help until something tragic happens. And that's when they contact my company.

So, what we try to do is educate adult children, and also the older population about what we do to serve them. And when people start changing their pattern, then that's the time to call and get us involved. Don't wait until the tragedies happen and you find yourself in the hospital and you need help, although of course, we do respond to that as well.

Because Linda's dad is very reluctant to move, one of the options she was considering is to just hire a caregiver to live with her parents and provide them both room and board. Her understanding is that it will be a less costly way of having someone with her parents on a regular basis. Bob provided input on that point:

I'm glad you brought this up. No matter who you're hiring or you're talking to, whether an agency and/or hiring somebody that's privately running an ad in the paper, and you've got somebody coming in the home, the things that you need to find out about is, number one is, did they have experience? I mean do they know how to do certain things because, if in fact they don't know how to do certain things, then they couldn't be effective and they could be hurting someone.

Secondly is, what kind of background do they have? In the case of hiring an individual, you can go down to your local government agency and ask to see if they would perform a background check. If you're hiring an agency, ask them, "Do you do a background check?" But don't stop there. Ask, "What type of background check?"

So, what you want to do is find out what kind of background check they're doing. What I look for is a company that's doing a background check that's going actually checking the county records seeing if this person has had any violation whether it's criminal activity, or going to the Department of Motor Vehicles to determine what their driving record is.

So that you really get a really good sense of who this person is because as you all know in the interview process, they are going to put their best foot forward because they want the job and will likely tell me what I want to hear. What I want is to see what I can find out about the potential caregiver. We do three different kinds of background checks. Number one is we do fingerprinting, which allows us to find out from the Department of Justice here in California whether that person has had any criminal activity.

We also do a national search, because if this person I'm talking to today and possibly hiring has lived in Alabama for the last ten years and just recently moved to California, my California background check with the Department of Justice is not going to tell me that. So what I've got to do is go and access a national database to find out what their activities were in Alabama. So that's important.

And my third is what kind of driving record? That's important because that gives you all kinds of different little signals. Because if you've got somebody who's consistently getting ticketed, well, what kind of judgment are they using? Because if they're consistently getting ticketed, then they're not using good judgment — will they use good judgment when they're taking care of your mom? And last but not least if they've got a pattern of drinking while intoxicated which shows up of course on their DMV, that's not a person you really want driving your mom around, either. So those are the kinds of things that I recommend.

The next thing is to make sure that the agency you're working with is an agency that employs the caregiver that they're talking to you about, because there are two different kinds of agencies that you could be talking to. There's one that's called the referral agency where you may be hiring a caregiver from them but in fact you as the homeowner become the employer.

In that case, then you're responsible for paying into their taxes. If they fall in your home and get hurt, you're responsible for their medical bills. I always believed, before I got into this business that, "Oh, when someone comes into my home and falls or gets hurt, I just call my homeowners, and my homeowners covers it." Well, that's not the case. Homeowner's states that if you have a person coming into your home on a one-time basis, your homeowner's, chances are, would cover that. But if you have someone consistently coming into your home and in this case taking care of your mom, then, in fact, your homeowners will not take care of that expense.

So there comes a liability that you've brought upon yourself by hiring somebody who has been consistently coming to your mom's home and they fell on the kitchen floor and hurt themselves. So you've got to be careful of that kind of thing.

Also, you don't want the government to come looking for you for any back taxes that may be owed if you are the employer of record. In the case of my agency, all of my caregivers are my employees. So, it's my responsibility to make sure that the taxes are paid, make sure they are covered under workman's comp.

Last but not least, you will want to make sure the person is bonded and insured, and those are different things. I always thought that maybe they're the same, but they are different If there's a problem in that the person covered in the home breaks something, then you want to make sure that they have insurance in order to cover the breakage or the loss of that.

Those are all things that need to be considered when you're hiring somebody to take care of your parents.

As you review home care agencies and find a big discrepancy in prices between agencies, chances are that the person, the agency you're talking to at the lower end is a referral agency. And all they're doing is referring a person to you. When you employ that person, they're your employee, not the referral agency's employee.

If you've got a company that's charging more money, then the reason why they're probably charging more money is because they are paying the taxes, because they are paying

workman's comp, and they are paying insurance as protec-
tion in case something goes wrong.

It may be prudent to consider a live-in caregiver if Linda's parents are going to both need 24-hour care at home. Even though that may not be the case at this time, she should align herself with a reputable in-home care agency. She now understands that, but wants to have a clear understanding as to the key differences between in-home care and having them go into assisted living. I talked with her about how each situation is different.

THREE C'S OF HOME CARE AND ASSISTED LIVING

Linda realizes that her parents are not as independent as they used to be and they need more assistance than they've had previously. The decision is whether to get someone to come into their home (more frequently) or having them move into a location that provides more supervision and care such as assisted living. Let's take a look at these two options in terms of care, costs, and cautions.

IN-HOME CARE

CARE — Most in-home care is non-medical care provided by trained caregivers. However, some home care can only be delivered by licensed, health care professionals. Caregivers can be hired through an agency, registry, or privately, and because every state has authority to license and regulate its home care agency system, there are often variations in licensure requirements and regulations from state to state.

COSTS — According to the Genworth 2015 Cost of Care Survey, the national range in the U.S. for non-medical care runs from $20-$40/hour (Median to Maximum). This is a huge range, and rates are different from one metropolitan area to another and rates are higher for medical or nurse assistance at home.

CAUTION — Caregivers can be hired from an agency or they can be hired as a private or independent caregiver. Be careful if you are considering hiring a private or independent caregiver, since the individual becomes your employee and you become the employer. On the other hand, if you hire an agency, they may be a little higher in cost but will screen caregivers and do thorough background checks, assume full liability for all care provided, supervise caregivers, cover auto insurance, take responsibility for caregivers' benefits, vacation days, and sick days and have a replacement caregiver available in case your regular caregiver calls in sick.

ASSISTED LIVING

<u>CARE</u> — Assisted Living options range from small, family residential care homes to larger, full-service communities with hundreds of residents. The smaller locations are similar to living in someone's home with caregivers who provide assistance 24/7. The larger locations (communities) are more like senior apartments with caregivers also providing 24/7 assistance. More and more seniors are becoming residents of specialized Assisted Living facilities including dementia care. Generally speaking, assisted living is for people that need help with the activities of daily living (ADLs). ADLs are considered the routine activities that people tend do everyday without needing assistance. There are six basic ADLs: eating, bathing, dressing, toileting, transferring (walking), and continence. If someone has some form of dementia, like Alzheimer's, there are locations that are licensed to properly care for individuals with this disease.

<u>COSTS</u> — According to the Genworth 2015 Cost of Care Survey, the median rate of an assisted living community (single, one-bedroom) was $3,600/month. This monthly base rate can range over $11,000/month for Alzheimer's and dementia care.

Regardless of size, base rate fees often cover only some of the total costs of needed assisted living services.

Communities will vary on the number of services that are included in the base rate.

CAUTION — There are many choices for those needing assisted living and/or dementia care and supervision. Selecting the wrong community or residential care home for your loved one can make things even more difficult. Consider using a local professional in senior care placement who is familiar with the various options, including care, costs and location. They can then suggest the best options for your loved one to continue to age in a safe place.

The MetLife Report on Aging in Place 2.0, *Rethinking Solutions to the Home Care Challenge*. states, "Although a large majority of older Americans say they want to age at home, it is often more easily said than done. Today's care infrastructure, technologies, existing housing, funding sources, and the businesses and services available are not being fully realized in order to achieve the promise most hope for as America ages." In addition, hiring in-home help may be a temporary fix for a permanent problem that will turn into being more expensive. Dementia will progress, and a person with dementia is going to become less functional and more needy over time.

Though most seniors want to stay at home, if they are going to be home alone just with a caregiver coming in at different times, social interaction is extremely important, especially with those suffering from dementia. In this type of situation, strongly consider adult day care in your community if in-home care is going to be the option that you choose.

ADULT DAY PROGRAMS CAN MAKE A DIFFERENCE

I felt is was important for Linda to know about adult day programs for her parents, and Amy Andonian has a background in adult daycare and the Institute on Aging has a program on adult daycare, so I asked her to talk to us a little bit about that. Amy explains what adult daycare is and how it could be beneficial for seniors to attend.

Adult daycare is very near and dear to my heart. It's kind of how I got my start in the field of aging. I started doing some volunteer work in the community, visiting both seniors in their homes as well as seniors in nursing homes at the VA setting. I was really frustrated and sad about how many seniors were stuck in their homes and didn't have the opportunity to get out there and stay connected to the community.

It seemed to be particularly worse when you were experiencing memory loss or any form of dementia, such as

Alzheimer's, and those were truly the most isolated and often depressed seniors I encountered. I thought there had to be another way. An adult daycare center is designed to provide care and companionship for seniors who need assistance or protective supervision during the daytime.

A lot of times these older adults might include seniors who are either in the early or later stages of memory loss, and those who are also experiencing increasing physical and mobility limitations. These daycare centers are essentially designed to provide socialization to these older adults so that they can get out of their homes, meet with other seniors, engage in physical activity and recreational activities, and just stay engaged. At the same time, what I came to learn is that these centers are equally as important for the family caregivers who are taking care of these older loved ones.

What these adult day centers are designed to do is to provide respite, which means a break, or a regular period of relief to family members and caregivers. It gives them the freedom to go to work, to take care of personal business or even just relax and take a break, while knowing that their older loved one is safe and well cared for.

A lot of times, caregivers find these centers too late and wish they had found them much, much sooner. What has been found is that these day centers can't stop the dementia from proceeding. It can oftentimes slow it down by keeping these seniors active and involved. It makes them feel better. It gives them a reason to get up every day and go to the center and still be engaged, while at the same time making sure that the caregiver continues to get the break and the support that they need.

It can be frightening. They don't often realize that it's happening, because they just continue to put their heads down and keep working and keep taking care of their own families and their older loved ones at the same time. That process can have some really long-term negative health effects.

When I started, I thought it was more about the senior and I just thought it was great — seniors can get out of their homes and socialize — but the more I became involved in the programs and the more I came to understand them, I came to think that the true client, the true person being served is really the family caregiver, because it allows them to keep their older loved one at home for a much longer period of time and that can delay institutionalization for the senior. And there are the emotional and quality of life benefits to that, as well as a financial benefit. Those are just huge for families.

Linda was concerned that if she talks to her mom or dad about all the benefits, what if they just don't want to go? Amy said this is very common and gave Linda this advice:

Give it time. Any change in routine can be incredibly difficult for an older adult, especially if they're experiencing memory loss and increased confusion. Chances are really good that if you find an adult day program and you enroll your older loved one, they're going to show some type of resistance when you go to actually drop them off the first couple of days or the first couple of weeks.

A lot of times this leaves the caregiver feeling anxious and guilty and questioning whether this is the right fit for their loved one and there can be a lot of emotions that come to the surface, but my advice is — and my experience kind of speaks to this — that usually over the first couple of weeks or so, the adult day program will gradually become part of your older loved one's new routine and they will come to expect it and often look forward to it.

I see so many families who after the first couple of days they think, "I can't do this. He won't get out of bed. He's dragging his feet and he just won't come." A month or so later, he's out of bed, he's sitting downstairs waiting, looking at his watch, saying, "We're going to be late. We need to go now." Once it becomes part of the routine, it's no longer scary. It's something they can actually look forward to and that becomes part of their day.

I also call for people to avoid calling it "daycare." A lot of times we just refer to it as "the club" or" school," and if you look at our website, we call It "adult day clubs." That really helps. If somebody is really resistant and maybe still a little higher functioning, they will notice that the other people in the program have more advanced dementia. A lot of times you can ease them into it by saying, "Well, you're just going to come and help us and volunteer and help the other seniors." That kind of empowers them. It makes them feel like they can give back in a way and then the program's there for them as their own dementia begins to worsen over the years.

I should emphasize too that there are two types of adult daycare. There's a medical model, which does provide a lot more care for the older adults, and there are social daycare programs more geared for folks who are experiencing memory loss, where the focus is on social activities, meals, recreation, and very minimal health-related services. They might give blood pressure checks every now and then, but really it's more about the socialization and maximizing what that individual can still do and still contribute in a group setting.

Whether Linda's parents continue to stay at home or live in any outside community, she will want to make sure that everything possible is done to prevent falls. When there are falls, many other problems can occur.

SIMPLE WAYS TO PREVENT FALLS

I asked Vanessa Kettler, creator, developer, and producer of Building Better Balance, to provide some techniques to Linda in order to help her parents improve their balance and prevent having falls. Vanessa provided the following thoughts:

As a caregiver, you can do a great deal to keep your parents from falling. Preventing falls will help them stay healthy, active and able to stay more independent.

- *Don't encourage talking with your parents while walking. They will tend to turn to look at you. Turning the head causes dizziness. Not looking where you are going is a recipe for disaster. It is very dangerous. Teach them to look where they are going. Walking requires full concentration.*

- *Encourage your parents to take all possible precautions if they wake up in the middle of the night and have to go to the bathroom. This is when balance is the worst and hazard is highest. Use the walker. Put on good shoes, not slippers or slip-ons. Make sure there is enough light. Make sure a path is available from the bed to the bathroom that your parents can hold onto. Do not expect balance to be ok in the middle of the night.*

- *Extended sitting is a big problem. Every hour of extended sitting reduces blood flow to the extremities by as much as 50%. Walking for 5 minutes each hour of extended sitting eliminates the trouble. Have your client get up once an hour to get a glass of water, go to the bathroom, or simply walk around the room. If walking is difficult, seated exercise can substitute. Foot exercises and leg stretches are great as are lower back releases.*

- *The most important thing you can do to help your parents avoid falls is to have them exercise regularly, with their doctor's approval, of course. The single action of establishing a consistent movement routine exponentially reduces the risk of falls. Participate in the workout along with your client. Try to keep to consistent scheduling.*

I explained to Linda that most falls are caused either by something foolish or something unexpected. By having her parents take balance classes consistently, even doing things that normally would cause them to fall become less risky. For example, if her parents learn to pick their feet up, they won't be as likely to trip on sidewalk cracks. Linda is signing them up for classes.

HOSPICE MYTHS AND REALITIES

Though Linda's parents are not on hospice, I wanted to introduce Linda to hospice so she can be familiar with it should her mom or dad ever go onto hospice. I introduced her to Paula Scoglio, who was chosen to enter the new graduate program at UCSF specializing in general medicine, oncology, and palliative care. Paula discusses the myths and realities of hospice:

The hardest thing about being a hospice nurse is to try to have families understand that if you could take away the word "hospice" and replace it with "symptom management" or "extra nursing care," everyone would want it. Because you're using the hospice word, people often equate hospice with immediate death, or they think about it as someone having morphine and just being drugged out before they actually leave this planet. I feel like there's a lot of fear surrounding the hospice word. Before I was a nurse I also felt that way. I felt like, "Oh, we're not ready for that yet." If someone would have explained it to me as, "A nurse is going to come to your house. You're going to have extra nursing care. We'll also have a nurse aide to help with the personal care of the person. Then you'll have social work come in. You'll have clergy come in if you so desire. We're just going to do that. Medicare's going to pay for everything." I would have said, "Yes. Okay. I'm in."

*You use the word "hospice" and people have a lot of miscon-
ceptions. I find that the most important thing I do, when
I'm talking to families is to try to help them understand
that, "Yes. According to a prognosis, it means that there's
a prognosis that if it ran its regular course possibly could
end up within six months. That's the prognosis of the person
has before hospice even enters." I would tell them that many
of our people graduate out of hospice because, with extra
nursing eyes on them, they do better. They no longer qualify
for the benefit that's paid 100% by Medicare.*

*Generally, how it works is that sometimes the family will
say, "Gee! I wonder if my mom should be on hospice or my
dad should be on hospice?" They can contact the company
directly. Always a physician has to write an order to evaluate for hospice. Then in admission, the nurse comes in and
they look at all the Medicare guidelines. They try to see if
there's any way the person can set the criteria so that the
benefit can be Medicare appropriate. Sometimes we look at
people and we say, "You know, not quite yet. At this point in
time it doesn't fit the guidelines. We can re-evaluate." Other
times we can say, "Yes. This falls in the criteria." However,
that does not by any means of the imagination mean, that
this person only has six months or less to live.*

*When you have hospice come in, they see any changes and
behavior and say, "Hey, maybe there is an infection." They
can treat them without having to go to the hospital, having*

to go the doctor's office, the emergency room, you generally have a wait time of hours and hours. The nurse can do that through the course of her visit.

Though most people don't want to talk about what could be the end for a loved one, I feel it is important for the entire family to understand more about hospice. Because being in hospice doesn't necessary mean an end, I wanted Linda to understand more, so I asked Paula to explain what is meant by the term "hospice graduate."

There are criteria that a patient or a person has to be evaluated every 60 to 90 days to see if the person still qualifies for the benefit. What that means is sometimes with hospice coming in, people do so much better that they are no longer "appropriate" for hospice. One of the criteria of having a hospice come in is weight loss of more than 10%. Say someone has been losing weight and then hospice comes in. Then they're starting to feel better. They're starting to eat better. All of a sudden, some of the things that were wrong with them that qualified them for the benefit, they no longer have. They started to gain weight and maybe they're starting to assist with putting on some of their clothes, or they're starting walk a little bit more because they're feeling better, and they're stronger because they're having nursing eyes on them all the time.

In those instances, after a 90-day period, the doctor comes out and takes a look at the person and says, "You know what? I think you're doing well. I think that you've graduated off of hospice. If you feel like you need us again, give us a call and we'll come in." Always, again, re-evaluating the patient.

Being on hospice does not mean that death is imminent. Sometimes that is the case, depending on when the person has chosen to look for hospice care. There were instances where I had one week where four of the people I saw were all people who had graduated off, and were being reevaluated. Sometimes the people don't even qualify for the re-evaluation. There are a lot of times when people are on hospice and they are so happy that the nurses are out looking in for them and taking the pressure off of the family that the family is really kind of sad that the person has graduated off in terms of not being able to get the nursing care that they are used to with hospice.

Part of the physician's role is to take care of the patient and to "cure the patient," to do everything that they can. I find that, often, doctors don't want to be the bearer of bad news. They don't want to say, "Hey, you know, I think your mom needs hospice," because they may feel like, "I don't want to give up on my patient. I don't want the family to think I'm giving up on them." We really have to do a lot of education of the doctors and the families.

Generally, the hospice discussion happens when there is an acute event. Say someone is hospitalized for something — pneumonia, urinary tract infections, maybe a fall. One of the criteria of hospice is how many hospitalizations has the patient had within the past six months. You look at that because it generally says something about their condition. Often, hospice stays are generated when somebody goes into the hospital for an acute event or ends up in a skilled nursing facility. The hospital or social worker or discharge planner may intervene and say, "Maybe we could see if this person is appropriate for hospice."

We do have some doctors who are very educated. They look at the situation and say, "Hey, I would like to get my patient extra help." Again, they can ask to be evaluated for hospice. I'm not finding the benefit being used as much as I would like to see it used.

If the doctors do write an evaluation and the patient is not appropriate, the hospice says, "This is not appropriate and the patient does not meet the criteria." Even if a doctor writes an order for an evaluation, it's up to our skilled nurses to decide — along with the doctor — whether the patient is appropriate for hospice or not.

Linda was concerned that if either of her parents had to go on hospice, that they would have to move to a hospice facility. I told her that though there might have been a time that people literally went to a hospice facility, that's not the case much anymore. I asked Paula to expound on that.

That is one of the myths that people have in terms of hospice being a place. Hospice is a service and the service is wherever you are, wherever you live. That is where we go. If you live in an assisted living, we go there. If you live in a board-and-care, which is a home to take care of people, we go there. If you are at home, we go there.

But if you're in a hospital, Medicare does not pay for hospice while a patient is in the hospital. There are some hospitals that have hospice-like units. For the most part, once you leave the hospital, then that's when hospice would start in skilled nursing facilities. There are hospice places, but there aren't very many of them.

Sometimes hospitals will have an area called "palliative care." With palliative care, they basically look at the disease process and they say, "This is a serious, serious illness." They're amazing, and they basically go in and talk to families and see what they can do for the patient. In that instance, they support all curative measures. When you're on hospice you basically have said, "I have tried all of the curative measures and it's just not working. I'm tired and I just don't want to do it anymore." During that decision, you say, "I'm looking at the quality of my life and I'm looking at comfort only. I really don't want to do anything curative because, you know what? I don't want to go to the hospital again. I don't want to go to my doctor visits. I just want to be home and I want to be with my family. I don't want to be in pain. I want to be able to breathe." All of these types of things, we take care of when the person is at home.

When you look at the palliative team, the palliative team says, "If you want any treatments, we will be supportive of that." It's different if you have a patient that is undergoing chemotherapy. If they wanted to continue to go through chemotherapy, the palliative team would be involved in that. When you're in hospice, hospice is more of a comfort. Chemotherapy can be really difficult to undergo. Chemotherapy generally is not covered under the Medicare benefit and the hospice area. There are certain decisions that you have to make in order to say, "Yes, I'm ready for hospice." The bottom line is that hospice care does symptom management. All your symptoms are taken care of. A palliative team can help facilitate other types of arrangements where somebody is actually still trying to undergo treatments that are more complex.

Along with the whole palliative care issue, sometimes people think choosing hospice means giving up all medical treatments. That is not the case. I mentioned chemotherapy because that is a very grueling treatment that is very hard on the patient and it does have side effects. Say for instance, you have a cardiac condition and you take blood pressure medications. Generally, hospices don't take away all of those medications. If you had something that was easily treatable and caused you discomfort, the hospice would treat it. If you had an infection, they could give you antibiotics for that infection as long as long as you could swallow, because swallowing is an important part of being able to take the antibiotics when you're in the home setting.

Say, for instance, you fell when you were at home and you were on hospice. Nobody is going to tell someone they have to just suck it up with a broken bone. That's not how it would work. You would go into the hospital and they would treat that, because that is not the nature of your illness. We want to make sure that our people are not in pain. That our people can breathe, that our people are not nauseous that our people are not agitated. It doesn't mean giving up on all medical treatments. It means giving up on aggressive medical treatment.

Hospice isn't just for the elderly. At the beginning they thought that hospice was just for cancer patients. Then they thought, "Oh, it's just for old people." Perhaps they even think that it's for the last days of life. In hospice, in order for it to do the best job that it can, the earlier we intervene for people, the better the patient can do. The longer they can be around for us, the more we can affect the quality of their lives. I'm a great proponent of saying, "If there's any criteria you think that you need, then you get extra help. You get nursing coming right to your door." I think that that is amazing. It really does help people have a better quality of life.

Sometimes families do it all themselves. They feel like, "I need to take care of mom and dad. It's my job." I understand that thinking. When you're doing all of that management, you take away one of the things that they need that only you can give them. That is you being the person you are to them. You let the hospice take care of all of the medical management.

When you let hospice come in, they have the medical eyes that you don't need to have anymore. You don't have to worry. You can just pick up the phone to the hospice and say, "Hey, I don't like what I'm seeing. Can you come and evaluate my mom or dad?" That's their job. Then you can go back to being the nurturing son, or daughter, or whatever parts you play. Only you can do that. We can give compassionate care but only you can be that person.

I felt it was important for Linda to know that hospice isn't just for the individual, it's support for the entire family. Paula commented on this point.

When you have a nurse come in, the nurse always sees how the family is coping. If they feel that they need any intervention or if the family says, "Hey, I'm having a tough time with X, Y, Z." Then they have the social workers that can come in and say, "These are the resources we have. This is the counseling that we have." Say, for instance, you're having an issue trying to figure out what you wanted. What's going to happen next? They have all of the resources to be able to put you in contact with all of the help you need. They're experts at it. That's all they do. We also have clergy. Clergy can come in and not only support the patient, but the family as well.

Sometimes, that makes all the difference in terms of how you're going to experience the experience. Generally, hospices have a year period where they support the family after their loved one has passed away. They are there for support because sometimes you need a little help, a little direction. And sometimes you need a lot, and they are there for that. That's also an excellent benefit that Medicare has put together. One of the things that Medicare has really done a great job with is hospice. I just wish more people could take advantage of it.

* * *

Linda realizes that if she had known a couple of years ago what she has learned by now, she would have done a much better job of communicating with her parents on these subjects versus avoiding talking about them: communicate, look at options, plan, and communicate some more!

CHAPTER FIVE

Enhancing Seniors' Lives Through Technology

Keeping seniors safe in every situation is very difficult. However, we have a far greater chance of keeping seniors safer than we did years ago. It's important for caregivers to have an open mind about new technology that is emerging at a rapid pace. Not only will this be a benefit to seniors but a benefit to family caregivers in so many ways.

MATCHING CAREGIVERS TO NEW TECHNOLOGY

Though Linda's parents are currently living at home, they are far from being independent. To try and keep them safe, they will either have to move to some type of assisted living, or receive care at home from a caregiver and incorporate some technology at home so Linda and her family will have some peace of mind.

To provide Linda with an overview of some technology to help support their loved ones, I connected Linda with Christina Irving, a licensed clinical social worker at Family Caregiver Alliance. Christina has conducted in-home caregiver assessments, teaching classes, making presentations on this important topic. Christina shared how technology can not only help seniors living at home but also assist the caregivers who are taking care of them.

There are lots of different ways technology can be useful. You can think about it as technology that supports the person needing care and then technology that supports the caregiver. The things that support the person needing care obviously help the caregiver as well. Some of it is really related to the direct care of the person in terms of the personal care issues that they need help with. Some of it is more around home safety and security issues.

There is also technology that helps provide emotional support and connection to the caregivers. Helping them connect with other caregivers, helping them coordinate care with other family members or with friends. It really covers different domains. Technology that helps with the actual physical care of the individual needing help, the safety issues, coordinating care and managing tasks and then providing the emotional support for the caregiver to help them manage their own self-care needs.

Keeping up with these new technologies is the biggest chal-
lenge right now because this is a constantly evolving field. A
lot of these companies haven't been around for a long time.
You can't use those old standards of reputation because they
may not have been in business for a long time. That doesn't
necessarily mean that it's not a good product or a good
service that they're offering. We don't have some of those old
standards for evaluating these products.

We encourage you right now to talk to other caregivers, talk
to professionals in the field, find out what they have used,
what people have tried. It's also about looking at what these
different technologies and products offer. It's not whether
this one is a good product but whether it's good for you.
There are so many similarities across different care-giving
situations but there are also differences. It may be a great
product or great service for somebody else. If it's not actu-
ally going to help you and give you the support and assis-
tance that you need, then it doesn't really matter how great
or innovative of a technology is it, it's not going to be useful.

I think starting there for caregivers to identify what are the
areas where they need more help, where are things stress-
ful or challenging for them and really having a good idea
of what it is that technology could do for them. Even if
you don't know what product or what technologies are out
there, just starting with, "What do I need? What's going
to make my life a little bit easier? What are the challenges

I'm facing right now?"...And then going from there to evaluate if it's helpful.

Unfortunately right now, there's not one repository of all the technologies that are out there. It is a lot of just searching, talking to other people, doing web searches. There are some good websites that have a number of different examples of information. That's really the best you can do right now in terms of getting a list of what's available. Listen to some examples because it will constantly change and there will be new things that will come up.

A couple other places for people to know to have a good repository or at least more detailed information about what's available. There's an organization called the Center for Technology and Aging that has some great information online. There's another group called the Tech Enhanced Life that has some great listings of technologies and products. Family Caregiver Alliance's website, we have some fact sheets and webinars based on technology and caregiving. There are some good places that you can find information. Just know that none of those are going to have every type of technology that is out there because there will be something new that will come out next week.

I asked Christina if there is a rating system of different technologies out there, like a Yelp, for these devices.

It's definitely too early right now to actually see a rating system. I know that's necessary for we're looking at. Again, these other agencies that I mentioned have a little bit of that but nobody right now has a Yelp for technology and caregiving. There is no one place for review sites.

You need to look at them carefully, looking at the details of information about them, evaluating it based on your needs, how the product works and the cost. Also, talking to other people is helpful. I think the more caregivers connect with other caregivers, with service providers and support systems out there, the easier it is.

Because this technology is so new, it hasn't been used by a lot of people. But when it's used, people do talk about it. Though you may not know somebody personally who has used these technologies, the social worker at the hospital or somebody at the caregiver support group might either have used it themselves or know somebody who has. The more people talk about it, the more you will get some of that feedback, but there's unfortunately no Yelp right now for it.

I asked her to share with Linda examples of some of the technology out there. Specifically, in Linda's case, for care coordination and managing tasks.

When we talk about care coordination or managing tasks, I think a couple of the sites that have been around the longest and really started its websites now, of course, have mobile apps as well. *Lotsa Helping Hands* is one that is commonly used as well as *CaringBridge*. Those two are great sites to invite family and friends to join around the person that you're caring for, to be able to have a calendar where you can designate different tasks that need to be accomplished and allow people to sign up for them.

There are ways to broaden your support circle a little bit and really engage those family and friends that may be around and offering, "Let me know if I can do anything," but not really doing anything. It's a way to help out whether it's people who want to be involved but live farther away or people who live locally but just need a little bit more direction.

They're pretty easy to use and fairly straightforward but then there are some other examples that get even more detailed. There's another site called *Cozi.com*, which is web-based but much more app-based. It really gets into tracking with the medication given, being able to have a shared shopping list so depending on who's going to go to the grocery store for Mom, different people can login and see this is what's needed that day. It allows you track appointments and then have people signup or have different tasks designated to different family members that are involved. There are a lot more details and it's really a way to engage and use the different people that may be involved in your loved one's life so that it doesn't just fall on one person to be the primary caregiver.

Those are some of the examples of the care coordination. When we get into more of the health management, I think the ones that people think the most frequently are the Fitbits or the Jawbones, that you don't really track your steps and manage your health in that way. There is a movement toward doing more of that healthcare monitoring. There are some physicians, particularly in rural areas that do use Telehealth where doctors are able to monitor blood pressure and blood glucose levels, where you can be transmitting that information with your doctor when you can't usually get into appointments.

But I think for just caregivers to use and purchase on their own, there's a lot of medication management systems. Some of those again are just apps, things like MediCoach, where you can put in what medications are needed and it will give you those reminders on your phone, "It's time for this dose, it's time for this dose. You're almost out of this medication, you need to refill it."

There are actual pillboxes that have alarms on them that will make a noise when it's time to take a medication that will lock if you haven't taken that medication within a certain time period so that you can't double dose or take medications too close together.

There are also pillboxes that will actually send an alert to someone's phone or email saying, "Yes, the pills from this particular time were taken out. They were taken out of the pill box." It doesn't necessarily say, "Yes they're absolutely taken by the person," but they at least indicate that the pillbox was activated at a particular time so they can get very detailed in that way.

Whether it has to do with technology or overall support, Linda can get support from various resources just with a phone call, phone applications, and various support groups.

In terms of caregivers being able to connect to get that emotional support, there are a number of online support groups. We have one, and the Alzheimer's Association has one. There are a number of places where you can connect with other caregivers, with people who understand what you're going through. We see this more and more — there have been Facebook groups for caregivers around specific diseases or health conditions. Those can be great ways for caregivers to get that support when you can't get out to a support group.

There are apps for meditation and relaxation exercises. Seldom people say, "I don't have time or I don't remember. I don't think about it. I don't know how to do it." There is an app called Breathe to Relax. Is takes you to some guided breathing exercises. That can be great thing for caregivers who know things like meditation and mindfulness are so helpful in managing stress and in helping with mood.

Finding just these simple apps or websites that can help you do that really can make a difference, mostly because they're easy for caregivers to do. We know they are really stretched, they don't have a lot of free time so when you can pull something out and do it on your phone for 5 minutes, it's a good thing.

Calm.com has both an app and is also online. You'll find some guided relaxation exercises for caregivers. That can be really helpful for managing their own mental health and their mood and getting support in that way.

Understand that most of the technology out there is to help support the system that's already in place as opposed to taking it over. Even the more high-tech technology of home safety monitoring services, where it may be a webcam or it may just be sensors that are monitoring the home to let you know whether somebody opens the refrigerator that day or they've locked their front door; those don't replace the need for a caregiver of some kind.

They provide more information, maybe give the caregiver a little bit more time off, they don't always feel tethered to the home, or even help with some of that worry and concern of, "Well, my mom's kind of doing okay but she needs a little bit of help. I don't know if anyone would be aware if she fell for two or 3 days. I just want to have more of a sense of security that she's doing okay."

Things like the home safety sensors can help with that. Again, it doesn't replace the need for having a caregiver present but it just may help them monitor safety and ease some of the worry and concern.

Linda brought up to Christina that she is considering a professional in-home care company to provide a caregiver to assist with her parents at home. She wanted to know if the agency would use some of this technology or is it geared more for family caregiving.

I think it's both. They often work in tandem. We know there are some seniors or people with disabilities who don't have family, who really don't have a big support system. They may be relying more on professional caregivers, on in-home help or case managers.

The technology can help somebody who lives a little bit more independently, who perhaps don't need as much help as they would if they didn't have any technology in place; however, it can also help those case managers or home care workers better support that senior, or the person with disability.

It can be used in both ways. I think it can be helpful for families and it can be helpful for the paid and professional caregivers. We know that many families will hire in-home help or will use a case manager because it often is more than one caregiver can do on their own and they need to get breaks, they need to get time away.

Sometimes these tools are actually useful in helping coordinate not only between a caregiver and other family members but also between a caregiver and paid professionals who are involved. We know that paying for in-home help or hiring a case manager is really only effective when there's good communication. When information is shared regularly and it's very clear "This is what needs to get done today. This is what Mom or Dad's care needs are," that information needs to be shared regularly. The technology can actually help with that.

Though this technology can be effective, I explained to Linda, as of right now, it's there to support a caregiver. We see information on robots replacing caregivers and what can they do. Right now, we're not there. We know there's so much that people gain from that person-to-person contact. Linda's parents need a person to care for them, even if it's just for the touch, for how much touch does for someone and how calming that can be.

I emphasized again that the technology it's there to help support the caregiver, too. When you can't get out so easily, there are online support groups. When you're having difficulty communicating and coordinating with your family, there are ways you can get help to do that.

SENSORS WATCHING OVER YOUR PARENTS

A new type of technology to help keep seniors safely at home are home sensors. I thought that this could be a support to Linda and her parents. I asked Mary Hulme, founder of Moonstone Geriatrics to speak with Linda about this technology. Mary is a geriatric consultant and co-authored an e-book called *The Home That Watches Over Your Parents: Activity Tracking Home Sensor Systems*. I asked Mary to further explain what the benefits are for home sensors.

As a social worker and as a care manager and consultant, it's my responsibility to keep up on any products that are on the market currently or coming out on the market that might be helpful for my clients and their families, and I've been very interested in technology. As is the case with Linda's parents, many older people do not want to move. They want to stay in their homes. A little over a year ago, I teamed up with my colleague, Dr. Richard Caro because we were both very interested in what technology was available or coming out that could help older people live safely at home. He and I both have 80-year-old mothers. He has a mother in Australia. I have a mother here in San Francisco.

As an overview, imagine if you will, that you have a home and scattered throughout the home are those sensors. You may have a sensor that you put on the refrigerator door, which tells you how often that door is being opened and closed. Or you may have a sensor over the stove that tells you when the stove is getting too warm or that area is getting too hot. Then you have an alert for an app on your phone. You might have a sensor on the front door or the garage door, which tells you when that door has been closed or more importantly when it's last been opened. These systems are sensors around the house that can monitor activity. They look for patterns and then if those patterns are not normal, or not what we expect, then they can alert someone.

For example, I have a client now who has dementia. There's a caregiver in three days a week, but the family can't afford to pay for more care. She is living alone and they worry that she might wander off or that she might fall. We have sensors set up on the house key that tells us when she leaves the house. We have a sensor on the front door that tells us every time that door is opened or closed. Then, we also have a sensor on her bedroom door, because every night when she goes to bed, she closes that door. If she is not up and out of bed by 9:00 AM, her son who lives nearby will get an alert through an app on his cellphone.

Linda was concerned that her dad would not like the idea that someone was watching every move he makes. She wanted to know if the seniors are actually aware of these sensors. Though she lives near her parents, she works a good hour away from them and wanted to know if response time could be an issue.

*As far as noticing the sensors, I put the sensors in my own
mother's house. She was certainly aware of it. We put
sensors in other older people's homes and they're aware of it
because sensors are quite discreet and not really noticeable.
We've discovered, and it has been interesting, that the older
people who live living alone and who are aware that they
have the sensors in their home, report feeling pleased that
someone is looking out for them from a distance.*

*I have a lot of adult children who say to me, "Well Mary,
let's just put video cameras in the house. Then I can keep
an eye on my mom or dad." There are a couple of problems
with that. First of all, none of my older clients are willing
to consider having a video camera in their homes. They
seem to forget is that you need to have somebody monitoring those videos. I can tell you, my adult children do not
have the time or the inclination to review every single day,
24 hours of video footage. My patients with dementia, who
are at risk of wandering or getting lost, do not remember
that they have the sensors and they don't notice them.*

*As far as response time if you're at work, maybe your parents
have neighbors that live nearby. Otherwise, the next step
would be to call 911.*

*Here is a true story about a woman and how the sensor
helped her: She was an 88-year-old living by herself. Quite
healthy, but her two adult children who did not live*

nearby were worried. They knew that their mom got up every morning between 7:00 and 7:30, so the son had the sensors set up. If she were not up and out of bed by 9, he would get an alert.

One morning, he did. He got the alert so he tried calling his mom. He could not reach her so he called a neighbor who had a key to the house. He asked the neighbor to go in. The neighbor went in and found her lying on the floor next to her bed. She was alert, she was conscious, but she could not move her left side. The ambulance was called. They learned she had a mild stroke. I like this example because it is a real story and these children, although they lived near their mom, only come by and visit maybe once or twice a week. Because she's so active and busy, when they call, if they don't reach her right away, they tend not to worry. What that tells us that without this home sensor system and without that alert going off, this lady may have been lying on her bedroom floor for an entire day or even two before anybody would have known that something was wrong.

Of course, so much depends on what you want these sensors to do, what job you want them to do. Do you want them to do everything? Do you want them to monitor every single time the refrigerator is opened or closed? Or do you want a type of system that has more of a watchdog function, that just lets you know if there are patterns that don't seem normal or that seem disrupted?

As it relates to sensors with Linda's parents, I explained to her that each situation is different. They might be similar, but certainly not the same. If it is determined that her parents can live at home, then the sensors may be a good support tool. However, this technology should not be the determining factor. You have to weigh out both safety and dignity.

A MIX OF HOME CARE AND TECHNOLOGY

As stated previously, Linda is considering, as an option, a way to combine in-home care with some technology to limit the amount of hours a caregiver would have to be with her parents. 24-hour caregiving is not going to be affordable. I introduced Linda to Seth Sternberg who is the co-founder and CEO of Honor. Prior to founding Honor, Seth was co-founder and CEO of Meebo, which brought instant messaging to the web and was then acquired by Google.

I asked Seth to explain why he went from a high-tech background to in-home care, and to provide an overview of Honor. Since Linda was already familiar with the in-home care agency model, she wanted him to also explain the uniqueness of his type of company, which is in business of caring for seniors at home.

The founders of Honor wanted to start a company where we could look an individual in the eye and know that we're actually making their lives fundamentally better.

While we were kind of brainstorming ideas for the next startup, I went and visited my mother in Connecticut. She picked me up at the airport and was driving me home. As she was driving me home, I noticed that she was driving a little bit slower than she used to drive. I just asked her, "Hey, mom. Why are you driving slow?" She said, "Well, it's now harder to drive than it used to be." That just got me thinking. What happens in five or ten years when my mom really needs help? I don't want to ever have to say, "Mom, you have to leave your home." I want her to always be able to be in her home.

If I looked around at how will I help my mom stay in her home, I discovered that 20 years after my grandmother passed away, nothing has changed. The process of going through my grandmother aging and then my grandmother passing away was really pretty terrible. We've really not advanced over two decades.

I went back to my founders and I said, "Hey, guys. I just found a really, really big problem, and we're all running right toward it. We need to figure out how to solve this." We started Honor with a mission of let's help our parents to be able to stay in their homes comfortably, with joy, and with grace as they age. That's what Honor is all about.

There are three fundamental differences. When we put Honor together, the fundamental thing for us was not actually to go into in-home care per se. It was to solve a problem. The problem being, how very hard it is to help your parents to be able to stay in their home as they age. In today's world, though there are some good agencies out there, as you said, some are good, a number of them are really not very good. The challenge is that as you are trying to find help for your mom and dad, it is very hard to know the reliably of those who can actually help you, who has great programs to help you, and who has your best interest at heart. The reason we went into private duty care is we felt that it was the area that actually needed the most help and where we could have the biggest impact.

Honor has been created with three very fundamental differences in the way it operates versus normal private duty care. The first one is just an absolute and complete focus on quality. In today's world, the paid care professionals are only paid on average that may be just above minimum. On average, they only get 20 hours of work a week and 56% of them are on welfare. Those people are not in a good place in their life to be able to take care of themselves much less someone else. We decided that to create great quality, we have to be able to pay the care providers dramatically more so that they could be in a good place in their lives in order for them to be able to provide great care; all the while not raising prices to the elders and on their families.

Our care professionals are paid considerably more per hour, which then lets us get the pick of a wide scope of care professionals. Then we're able to select the absolute best and then those are the ones who make it on Honor's platform. Quality is piece number one.

In our case, technology does the matching between the very heterogeneous needs of seniors and the very heterogeneous capabilities of care professionals. If you think about it, your mom's needs and my mom's needs are different. The capabilities of care professionals are very different. We have a very wide pool of care professionals to pull from. We match their unique capabilities with the unique needs of your mom and dad. That also leads to substantially better quality, too.

Then there's convenience. It's impossible to get a care professional to come in two hours or to reliably come in two hours at X time. We focus a lot on convenience. You can literally just call our 800 number, download an app, go to our website and say, "Hey, I need someone. I need them here now." Almost always in the San Francisco Bay Area, there will be someone there in two hours. Convenience is another really big piece that we shoot for. Like I said, you can schedule online.

At the user level they get an app that shows them who's going to their mom's house or who's coming to their own house if they're getting care for themselves. It lets them talk to that care professional. It lets them see that Mary went to this per-

son's house today, went to her mom's house today. This is what Mary did in my mom's home. It lets you rate Mary. It lets your mom rate Mary. It's about giving the user more visibility and more control, really simple scheduling like we were talking about before.

Fundamentally, for the users, Honor is a service. It helps you or your parents stay in the home as they age. There's a lot of technology in the background that's doing things like efficiently scheduling to make sure that we can actually get someone to your home very quickly in just a couple of hours. It's a terrible thing to us if someone is ever late. This technology is doing the matching of the kind of needs of the elderly person with the capabilities of the care professionals.

There's a lot of technology that's all about making Honor, just this service, fundamentally better like giving you someone that's higher quality, and even letting us pay people more. The technology makes us more efficient and that's how we're able to pay care professionals more without having to charge more to the families. Families can pay the similar prices to what they're paying while the care professionals are paid more. There's a lot in the background there that makes our service fundamentally better.

I wanted Seth to explain more to Linda about how he can keep rates competitive with others while paying the caregivers at a higher rate.

Sure. One example is we don't need schedulers. We don't need people who sit and figure out where care professionals are and when they can get to a certain place. We can just tell all that by technology. It's just all handled in a microsecond by a computer. We can route people more efficiently so we can make sure the care professional ends up going to appointments or are scheduled for appointments that are closer to given geographic area to be more efficient. There's a lot in just the operations that allow us to be more efficient because we're using technology rather than having to have humans do those tasks.

A good example is, in a traditional agency, we found out something that was pretty distressing from the care professionals that were onboarding Honor. We showed them the button in our app that they hit when they're sick. When you're sick, you have to hit this button, so that we know you're sick, and then our technology will automatically find a replacement for you. The care professionals were completely amazed by that. They were going gaga over it.

In our case, they hit the button that says, "I'm sick." Then a computer in a micro second backfills them with someone else who's the next best match as opposed to what a good agency would do, which is going down a phone tree. They'd have someone sitting in the office who literally starts just quickly dialing a lot of different care professionals saying, "Are you available? Are you available? Are you available?"

This is a very people-oriented business. This is an operationally intense business. There's so much in there that a computer can just do better than a person can while, of course, recognizing that sometimes the computers can't do it. Honor is designed so that if it finds something where it says, "You know what? I need help." "I'm not sure if I have the best match for this senior. I don't know if I can find the best care pro. The computer will actually tell one of Honor's people, "Hey, I need help now."

Honor's platform works so a care professional can say, "You know what? I only want to work these days and these hours." Maybe it will amount to ten hours a week because maybe it's a stay-at-home mom who's normally with her daughter. She has these ten hours every week that are available to work on Honor's platform. Well, that also meaningfully increases the number of people who are available to be care professionals for seniors. If you're able to dynamically apportion labor, apportion care professionals, then you can dramatically increase the population of people who are care professionals.

We bring a lot of people into the profession of caregiving in order to serve the needs of seniors over time. We have some really, I think, fascinating concepts internally which we're not really talking about yet externally. They're about how you take people and time, today isn't really an issue from the scale perspective. How do you find people who fit the profile of someone who could be an amazing care professional? You

test them and you know that they can be amazing care pro-
fessionals. How do you get them training that's not just in
a classroom but real world kind of experiential learning?
That's what I'm really excited about. In time, we'll start
looking at those kinds of things.

Linda is considering Honor in her search for in-home care agencies. I did tell her that though technology is important, matching up the right caregiver for mom and dad is essential. Of course, caregivers can get sick and having back-up immediately is important, but the primary caregiver for her parents is probably the most important part of this transition.

* * *

After meeting with Linda about these issues of technology to support caregivers, she decided she would spend some time getting clearer about what combination of technology and caregiving would be the best fit for her and her parents.

Within a few weeks, she came up with some technology that would warn her father when her mother tried to get up from her chair or bed to try to walk without assistance. This helped decrease the chances of her mother falling again. Once Linda's mother gets stronger, hopefully she can remove that technology.

CHAPTER SIX

Protecting Your Parents from Abuse

FINANCIAL ABUSE OF ELDERS

A stranger suddenly wants to be your mom's BFF. An elderly client at the bank where you work comes in one day to withdraw an inordinately large sum of money. A financial advisory firm invites your elderly parents to a free lunch. All of these are red-flag moments — events that call for further investigation to protect seniors from financial fraud. Linda's parents are both open for exploitation, and it's important for Linda to hear more details to minimize the chances of this happening with her parents.

Shirley Krohn, a senior assembly member with the California Senior Legislature (CSL) and tireless worker devoted to fighting senior exploitation expressed her thoughts to Linda about this issue.

I would say, don't go to any free lunches, and if you do, don't talk to anybody. Get your lunch and leave. It's a huge issue and it's getting bigger every day. In fact, I would call it an epidemic, all the way from the financial scams, to the lottery scams, to the family members and caregivers taking advantage of seniors. It really is a nasty situation not just in California. It's all over the nation and I've even heard about situations arising in other parts of the world. Even in our sovereign nations, the tribal community, they are experiencing this as well. There is no sacred ground anymore or safe place for anybody. It makes it that much more important for people to be aware of what they can do to protect themselves.

The biggest perpetrators of these crimes are family members and/or caregivers, which is a huge issue, because family members can do things to isolate a senior so that they don't have any outside communication. Caregivers can do this as well. With family members it starts out on a congenial level, and then over time they get access to the checking account or to a credit card or some such thing.

There are also instances when a family member or a caregiver could place a senior in isolation so that they have no contact, whatsoever with people outside of their immediate surroundings. I've even heard stories where people are locked into a bedroom and that's where they stay until they're given something to eat, if indeed they're even fed. It's a pretty horrific crime.

We all know it's a problem, but most people don't know how big a problem it is. According to the government, 2.9 billion dollars a year are stolen from elders, and a more recent study done by a private organization put that number at 36 billion dollars a year.

Of course, with the population expanding, it's not going to get any better. Education and awareness are two primary ways we can combat the crime. I don't know that we're going to stop the crime, but at least we can get some awareness out there.

There is no economic cutoff as to when people can be victimized. The big picture if you look at it is that the aging older generation holds almost all the major equity, most of them in their own homes, maybe even out right. They've got equity built up, and that becomes a very big target for a family member or a caregiver.

Carolyn Rosenblatt, who we spoke to earlier about dealing with family fights relative to aging parents, also has had experience in dealing with financial abuse within families. Carolyn offered this information when we spoke to her earlier:

One of the reasons this is such a rampant issue is because of the relationship adult children have with their parents, especially if the parent was highly educated, or very successful, or very powerful, or intimidating.

I'll give you an example. This gentleman, whose family I worked with, had been the CEO of a company and was described to me as a tall, handsome, intelligent, imposing figure, always in control of everything. Well he developed dementia. He was placed in a fancy assisted living facility, and he was very lonely, he was widowed, and one of his caregivers decided she was going to make the best use of her role with him. She got very seductive with him in terms of being overly friendly, and the next thing we knew she had convinced him to wire $10,000 to her boyfriend in a foreign country.

That is an example of financial elder abuse, at multiple levels. The family was not paying attention to the caregiver — client relationship, which was out of line; you don't get that close to somebody you're taking care of in an institution, because you're an employee there. The family wasn't monitoring very closely, the facility certainly wasn't monitoring very closely, and anybody who would let this caregiver take this guy out of the facility, go to the bank, and do a wire transfer, there's something wrong with this picture. Now it isn't always that blatant, but the family members had a lot of trouble confronting their father about this. They were intimidated by him.

One of them was a professor at a law school, so the family's own ability to stand up to their dad goes back to their relationship with daddy from childhood. They were afraid of him. It doesn't matter how accomplished they are in their lives, how much they know about the law, it's still about dad, and the kids, and roles that they have played in the past that may stop them from doing what common sense would tell them is necessary. That's one aspect of it. It's just fear, or people are seduced into thinking that everything's okay because it's dad and he's really smart.

Elder abuse has been studied pretty much by a lot of different entities, insurance companies, the government, elder organizations, a lot of research has gone on to try to get to the bottom of why this problem is so massive, and why it's growing.

There's no one answer, but families are the most frequent abusers of elders when it comes to finances. They have the opportunity, and that's the reason. If a grandson, for example, who is beloved by grandmother, wants money, or has a drug addiction problem, or whatever it is, knows that he can manipulate his grandparent because of that trusting relationship and that love, that grandson can take advantage of grandma very easily. The same is true with adult children and their parents; it is true with other relatives, sisters, brothers, financial abuse by family members is a huge problem.

When you look at the statistics about who else steals from elders it's interesting. Family members are the most frequent abusers. Caregivers and people familiar to the elder — like the gardener, the secretary, whoever — are the second most frequent abusers, also because of opportunity and the trusting relationship. But the most money, as a chunk, is actually stolen by professionals. Financial advisors, lawyers, insurance brokers, all kinds of people who are in a position to know how much money and how to get it.

I have seen some things that are horrifying. The legal profession is very much against the selling of what we call variable annuities to elders. There is a really strong move in the legal field to try and protect clients from getting sucked into buying those. There are a lot of things to say about them, but generally speaking they tie up the elder's money for many years, 10 years, 12 years, really long time. It provides an income, but the problem is, let's say, an 80 year old person just got some variable annuities and tied up a bunch of their money, then they fall and break a hip, go in the hospital, come out, need care at home, want to stay at home, can't afford to pay the caregiver because their income isn't sufficient to do that.

They can't get the money out of their annuities without paying a huge penalty. That's where it falls apart in terms of being a good idea. The people who sell them make a huge commission, and that is the incentive for them to sell these people, to elders, and they have all sorts of justifications for doing so. That's where financial advisors take advantage, broker dealers, I should say, in particular, because they do not have what we call a fiduciary obligation to their client. They have only what's called a suitability standard, and that's kind of a joke.

Suitability only means it's okay that the institution makes money, and you could buy something that would be better for you. It is not something that is necessarily what is best for the client. Among financial professionals, only those with what we call fiduciary standard must do what is best for the client. That's only about 10% of the industry. The majority of people in financial services are advising our aging parents and grandparents in a way that is not necessarily best for the client. One of the things you ask is what can we do to protect them. I think we need to be doing a lot more looking over aging a parent's shoulder than we ever did in the past.

Linda has had some issues with her dad in the past that carry on into her current relationship with him. She is scared of him, not from a physical standpoint but he has become verbally abusive. She believes her brother and an outside organization are taking advantage of him financially, but she doesn't know for sure and is scared to ask either of them about it. Carolyn offered a perspective that would require Linda to have the courage to step up in order to try to protect her parents' financial situation.

Yeah, there's the rub. I think it goes back to the fear people have of the relationship with their parents. Their parents were in charge, and the children feel it would be disrespectful, that maybe they need to honor their parents' independence.

I've heard every excuse in the book about why people don't step in, and I say sure, you just honor their independence right into bankruptcy, while other people rip them off because you do not have the guts to stand up and say, "Dad, this doesn't look right. Maybe we both need to look at this together." Or, "Dad, I'm really concerned about the amount of activity that I'm seeing you do on the Internet with people you don't know. I really want to help you, can we talk about it?"

Shirley and Carolyn bring up approaches that Linda needs to implement with her father. If she sees this going on, then "honoring his independence" is just an excuse and she cannot hide behind it. With this new information, Linda felt more willing to bring up the financial issue with her father and brother.

SENIOR SCAM PREVENTION

We have discussed issues with Linda that have already taken place. Though they have to be dealt with, how can scams be prevented in the future? Art Maines is a licensed professional counselor and expert in frauds and scams against the elderly. Art is the author of *Scam: 3 Steps To Help Your Elderly Parents & Yourself.* He has trained on topics related to elderly fraud recovery and prevention to professional groups and senior organizations and has consulted with scam victim's family, locally and nationally. Though Art has become a specialist on this subject matter, this can happen to anybody, and I asked him to share with Linda the personal experience he had which led to him writing his book and dedicating himself to this issue.

Well, fortunately or unfortunately, it was personal experience to do with my stepfather, Bill, who was a wonderful man and was part of my life for 46 years. I actually knew Bill longer than I knew either of my birth parents. When he moved to St. Louis, where I lived back in 2006, I had told him about the prevalence of scams in the world and told him to be sure to check with me if anything sketchy or questionable showed up either by the phone or by email. I didn't continue talking to him about it, but and then in June of 2009, what came to light is that he had been getting ripped off for about five months by scammers with a phony sweepstake scam. And he didn't get the whole thing stopped until a police detective and a uniformed police officer from the town he lives in confronted him at the grocery store courtesy counter where he had been wiring money overseas to crooks. He lost just over $70,000. That's a terrible scam.

I'm such a social worker at heart. I'm all about helping people, and so about a month after this all came to light with Bill, I had a sort of a social worker epiphany, and I though, well, I'm learning about how elders recover from scams and how to help them recover from scams, so maybe this could help other people, and one thing led to another, and I ended up writing a book, despite the fact that I'd never thought about doing it before.

It's important for Linda to know that everybody in this country has a big target on their back. I mean, children are the victims of identity theft. Certainly, a lot of scams affect younger people. But, elders have some different kinds of vulnerabilities. For example, people over 50 in this country control 70% of the nation's wealth. So scammers know that folks over 50 are where the money is. But elders may also have some level of cognitive impairment, either through dementia-type illness or over medication. Sometimes they are not as security-conscious as I would hope, because — like Bill said to me — he was raised in a time and place when people were trustworthy. I mean, certainly there were con artists, but you wouldn't think they were as common and as viciously predatory as they are today. You may also have somebody who isn't as aware of the increasingly sophisticated electronic forms that show up via the Internet and the computer. So, there's a whole host of reasons that elders can, but don't have to be more vulnerable.

I asked Art to share how these predators are finding seniors and what steps he would recommend to help prevent these scams.

A lot of it is through the phone book or online telephone listings. They're looking for older-sounding names. If you see someone named Helen or Herbert they're more likely to think that's an older person than someone named Justin or Tiffany, for example. So, they will target people based on names. They will target people based on the part of a country. There are a lot of scammers specifically working in places like Florida and Arizona, and other retirement havens. So, they look for whatever they can to find them. A lot of times, it's just cold calls during the day, because scammers know that elders tend to be home during the day.

Making seniors aware of these scams is the best way to help prevent them. I'll talk about some of the newer ones because when I go out and give my talks, I try to give people the most up-to-date information that I can about scams that are affecting certainly my area right around St. Louis, but certainly also happening all over the country. There's a new scam which is an electronic form that is spoofing or mimicking a funeral home. Now, the original example of this came from a funeral home in Texas. The scammers are so good at what they do, and they know that email users are increasingly savvy about spotting these sorts of questionable messages. So, they're looking for ways to have people evade the delete button. So, a scam email is making the rounds that look like a funeral notification. And so what will happen is an email will show up with the subject line, "Funeral Notification," and it looks exactly like the logo and colors for a specific funeral home. Now, it isn't limited just to funeral homes, this is just where it all started. And it will say, "You'd been invited to a celebration of your friend's life service" on a given date. "For more information, click here," and that link will take a person, either to a site where their personal information could be stolen, or it would download malware and spyware into their computer that would go and look for usernames and passwords.

So, the scammers are trying to build credibility and evade our powers of critical thinking and skepticism by appearing to be a legitimate, even desirable, kind of business or invitation. That's one that has various permutations and styles now. There's another one that has prompted me jokingly to say, okay, I have to write a revised edition of the book, and that is, scammers are pretending to be the police or say a state highway patrol or something like that calling. And on a person's called ID box it will show the number for Missouri State Police or something like that. And they'll call up and say, "Hey, there's a warrant out for your arrest and we want to give you the chance to handle this right now over the phone. So just give us your bank account number, your debit card number, or go get one of those pre-paid *cards like a green-dot card, and let's just take care of that right now." That will get your attention if somebody calls up and says you have a warrant out for your arrest. And the caller ID box says whatever local police department or the FBI or even the IRS. So, they'll be more likely because of the credibility factor to fall prey to the scam. So, the scammers are working hard to keep evolving their methods based on credibility to get people to fall for the scams.*

Underpinning all this is emotional manipulation, which gets into the psychology of scamming. So in this case, the scammers are using fear, the fear of some sort of prosecution or outstanding warrant to get people to lower their guard and part with either personal information or money or both. Grandparent's scam is about fear and sympathy. A person is afraid that their beloved grandchild is stuck in some Mexican jail or something. So, they want to help them out and they will part with money and wire it to some offshore location.

As far as prevention, I break it down into what I call the 3R's. We've all heard about the 3R's of old-time education, which is reading, writing, and arithmetic. I think in the world of scam prevention, to be really effective at it, there are 3R's involved. The first one is recognize. You've got to recognize when a scam is coming your way. And to that end I talk about dead-giveaways for a scam. This would be things like having the scammer choose you in any way.

The email comes in, and they're choosing you! A phone call comes in, and they're choosing you! Or it could be someone who's very nice and charming, the scammer may tell you to keep secret the actions they're asking you to carry out. I've got a list of 10 or 12 of these dead-giveaways for a scam. So, it's recognizing a scam coming your way.

Knowing what to do is next, which is the respond piece and that boils down basically to boundaries. But, you've got to know what to do with what's called a "ransomware scam," something that pops up on your computer and hold your computer hostage and you got to know what's going on when somebody comes up to you in a parking lot and tries to get you to go with them because they found all this money which is the beginning of what they call the Pigeon Drop. So, you have to know the right ways to respond.

And, finally, you've got to know how to reach out. I say, "Reach out to check it out," or "Reach out and tell other people" about the scam, because that makes you feel good because you're helping other people.

It boils down to those 3R's: recognize, respond, and reach out.

Linda said she's going to brief her parents and others after hearing these examples and the 3R's, but she wonders what if it really is happening to her father? W asked Art what he suggested they do? Hang up the phone or get some info that they might help catch these people out there? Art provided his recommendations.

Well, generally, it would be to hang up the phone. However, there are some stories that I've heard and shared with seniors about different elders who have messed with the scammers a little bit. There's this whole world that's called scam-bathing," and there's this one lady that I talked to who got a grandparent-scam call. This scammer said, "This is so and so, I'm an attorney representing your grandsons, Will, Paul, and Charlie." And she said, "Oh, honey, you must have the wrong number because I'm a retired nun."

So, she messed with him that way. But, generally you want to hang up the phone. If you can get a phone number to call them back, it would be helpful. But, you don't have to be a police officer to take care of yourself. I recommend after you hang up the phone, the next phone call is to your local police, because they need to know that this stuff is going on. Now, of course, different police departments will be more responsive than others. But, in general, the local police that I've talked to all want to know about this because they want to look out for the elders in their community.

Scams against seniors are one of the most devastating types of scams or financial exploitation or abuse, because of the betrayal piece. A person has a hard time believing that someone who's supposed to be caring for them and even *loving them would perpetrate such a terrible thing against them. And so there's a high level of disbelief. There can also be a reluctance to prosecute because of the effects on the family. But, it's often a crime of opportunity and desperation because, within those families, there is at least one person who is what we would call "under functioning."" And these are the people who can never quite get it together: maybe they struggle with addiction or depression or a chronic under-employment, which plagues so many people in this new economy. And so, out of desperation, they will start to take money from their grandparents. And it goes on, and it goes on, and it goes on. And it becomes what we call "account dripping," where a person takes a little money from the grandparent over time, repeatedly. There's also what AARP has aptly termed the "Well, okay" syndrome, which is where the under-functioning younger person will come to the grandparent and say, "Grandma, I need a $100 to pay for my car insurance." And grandma goes, "Okay" because she wants to help. But then that person comes back a month later, and says, "Well, I need $200 now for my cell phone bill." And grandma says, "Well, okay." And then, well okay, well okay, well okay becomes grandma doesn't have enough money for food or medicine because the under-functioning person is playing on her sympathy and draining her dry.*

This information and advice was an eye-opener for Linda. Though she doesn't want her parents to worry all the time about scams, she plans for these issues to be a topic of conversation with them.

* * *

I advised Linda to not only share what she is afraid of about her brother and other third-party financial irregularities on her father's account, but she also needs to have a heart-to-heart discussion about scam prevention, or this type of situation can happen again. Linda agreed, and we talked a while about how she could take care of herself through the process.

After some additional research, Linda typed out (in large font) some of the most prevalent scams and put it near each telephone in her parents' home.

CHAPTER SEVEN

Taking Care of YOU

According to the Family Caregiver Alliance, "the psychological health of the family caregiver is negatively affected by providing care. Higher levels of stress, anxiety, depression, and other mental health effects are common among family members who care for an older relative or friend."

Whether you are providing or coordinating the care, taking care of a parent, spouse, or another loved one can put tremendous stress on your body. It has been quite clear to me that Linda is stressed with not only handling her parents' situation but also taking care of her own family and working on top of that. If Linda does not take care of herself, she will become another statistic, and statistics show that the stress of caregiving can cause a higher chance of physical and emotional illnesses.

THE SILVER TSUNAMI

I spoke to Jay Olshanksky, who received his PhD in Sociology at the University of Chicago in 1984. He has been a Professor in the School of Public Health at the University of Illinois in Chicago, and research associate at the Center of Aging at the University of Chicago and at the London School of Hygiene and Tropical Medicine.

The focus of his research to date has been on estimates of the upper limits to human longevity, exploring the health and public policy implications associated with individual and population aging, forecast of the size, survival, and age structure of the population, pursuit of scientific means to slow aging in people, and global avocations of the re-emergence of infectious and parasitic diseases.

Dr. Olshanksky is on the Board of Directors at the American Federation of Aging Research, and is the first author of *The Quest for Immortality, Science at the Frontiers of Aging*. I shared my conversation with Linda after Dr. Olshansky and I spoke.

People are living longer on average, and Linda's parents are no exception. They warded off other challenges, like cancer and heart disease, that may have killed either of them in times past. As some of us in the industry refer to it, the "Silver Tsunami" is hitting right now. People kind of laugh it off a little bit, but I think it's a serious issue and I'm concerned not only about whether we're ready in this country for it, but if we're ready around the world. I asked Jay his thoughts on this matter.

In terms of this concept of Silver Tsunami, there's a tendency of many people to look at this aging of the population in a negative light, to be fearful and scared, and at one level that's valid. If you were essentially standing on the shoreline looking at a population heading towards you, the Baby Boom generation, born between 1945 and 1964, is just now hitting the shoreline. That's why they're calling it a tsunami. There are roughly 10,000 people turning 65 every day for the next 15 to 20 years. So, the number of people who are going to reach older age is huge, and it is growing very rapidly. Now, on the one hand, we can look at it at it in a positive light. There's going to be a significant impact on age-entitlement programs like Social Security and Medicare. Please don't look at it only in a negative light. You can also view the aging of the population and the life expectancy we're enjoying in a positive light. We should be enjoying the success of advances in public health and medicine that have gotten us this far.

When we talk about aging, think of it in two ways. They're related but we need to distinguish between them. One is "life extension," which is living longer. The average lifespan was about 50 at the beginning of the 20th Century. It is now closer to 80, and for women it's even a little bit higher.

"Population aging" refers to the number of old people reaching ages 65 and over. That's related, but you can actually have a decline in life expectancy and an increase in population aging at some places — that's exactly what's happening. So, we're in a very unusual demographic event that we're facing now and the bottom line is most countries are not prepared for it. In fact, most people who are aging now, especially the Baby Boomers, have not prepared themselves adequately for the number of years they are likely to be spending in retirement. That's why you see these interesting advertisements, for example, from the insurance company Prudential, which has these wonderful ads illustrating that most people don't really have a concept of how much longer they're going to live after they retire and what the consequences of that are. Alerting people to the degree to which these changes are occurring, how much longer they're going to live, how to prepare for death — that's what we're dealing with now.

If you lived to 85 or 90 years old and no one really had to take care of you and you don't wake up one day, that's one thing. But I work with families every day who are just like Linda's family, whose parents both have challenges. Her mother has been diagnosed with dementia and, financially, they're not in a great position for the type of care they need today and will probably need in the future.

There are so many people out there who need supervision, who need care, who don't have the dollars to be taken care of in the way they should be, and that's a scary thing.

Linda's family wasn't prepared for this. From a bigger picture standpoint, is our country ready?

The answer is: no we're not. We face an unusual dilemma. We got exactly what we wished for, which is longer life. We reduced the risk of infectious diseases early so we live longer. We're now saving people from dying from cardiovascular diseases and cancer with much greater success. You have to realize that in the world of aging, death is a zero sum game. That means that if we lower the risk of death from one disease, something else must rise, because death is inevitable in all living things. So, in humans for example, when you lower the risk of heart disease and cancer, you expose the person saved to the population saved to an elevated risk of other diseases. You mentioned one of the most critical ones that we're concerned about and that's dementia, Alzheimer's and related conditions. That's what we're not prepared for.

I think many people don't quite realize what the consequences of success are if we continue to go after a major fatal diseases as we have. I'm not saying we shouldn't, by the way. What I'm saying is we face a very unusual dilemma and what we do know is that Alzheimer's disease and other related dementias are on the rise and able to rise dramatically in the coming decades. So, people are not only going to be exposed to the risk for a longer time period. They will experience these diseases for a much longer time period. I think a lot of folks are simply not aware of it and certainly not prepared for it. We have to be aware that these changes are forth coming.

I saw something recently from the *Alzheimer's Association*. It's been talked about that Alzheimer's is the sixth leading cause of death. However, those numbers are increasing dramatically, while other causes of death, like cancer and heart disease, are decreasing.

I interviewed a scientist recently who said that the likelihood of finding a cure for someone with Alzheimer's is pretty remote, at least in our generation. What they're concentrating on is trying to prevent people from getting it in the first place. I asked Dr. Olshansky what his research shows.

Well, that researcher is right. Look, people who already have Alzheimer's, like Linda's mother, are not likely to experience the reversal in their lifetime. The science is not far enough advanced to essentially reverse damages that already occurred in the brain or which have accumulated in the body, to say the body is just aging in general, by the way.

We're not going to be reversing aging or growing younger. The likelihood of reversing Alzheimer's Disease is extremely remote. There are a lot of folks who already have it. So, for them they've got a very difficult road ahead. Is there a prospect for preventing it entirely? Right now there isn't anything in the pipeline. But there are researchers working on it. I think that's probably where their focus is, appropriately, so trying to find a way to delay the onset or prevent it all together, or at least lower the symptoms associated with it. Actually, there is something that we can do now. We know at least the evidence has began to emerge that can influence the rate of progression of Alzheimer's disease.

There are two things actually; one of which is basic education. Believe it or not, acquiring an education, the more that you have the better off you are in terms of either delaying the onset or the progression of the Alzheimer's disease, and perhaps more importantly, addressing the consequences associated with having it. The other factor that seems to influence it to some degree, where there is marginal improvement, is exercise. Exercise seems to be the only equivalent of the fountain of youth that exists today and has a positive effect on just about everything. But don't hold your breath on anything that's going to deal with Alzheimer's for people that already have it. I'd be very cautious about claims that we're going to be preventing it anytime soon.

Let's talk about physical exercise. I plan on sharing your thoughts with Linda, so can you provide a little more detail what statistics show. I mean, should someone be running, walking, should they be doing weights? What do you recommend?

It varies from one person to the next. Some people are incapable of running, some people shouldn't be running because of injury to their knees and hips that occur during the course of their life. But the bottom line is, you need to treat your body in very many ways like you treat your car, at least the way you should treat your car. You take it in for an oil, lube, and filter frequently, you know it runs better when you do that. You take it in for a tune up, you know it runs better when and you do that. The same thing applies to your body. If you treat it right, you feed it the right kinds of food, you exercise your body, you're increasing the chances that you can live a healthier and longer life. Let me be real though. Even if you do everything right, I don't want this to sound negative, but it's the reality, you eat right, you exercise, you reduce your intake of calories, we still grow old. That's still going to happen. In all likelihood, we'll still get diseases associated with aging. Hopefully, they will be delayed or compressed in a short duration of time near the end of life. But the whole idea is to enjoy life for as long as we can for as healthy as possible. The benefits of exercise, let me be crystal clear on this, are instantaneous. We're not talking about to wait a day or week or a month or a year for benefit.

Regardless of what age you are, whether you're 20, 60, 80, or 100, you should be exercising. That can be as little as walking, just being vertical: walking, moving, gardening. Any of those physical activities that involve movement are critical. When you're horizontal for any extended period of time, that's when you run into trouble. So, any kind of movement is good. Weight bearing exercises are wonderful. Anything that gets the heart rate up is great. Remember, it's going to vary from one person to the next. So, the first thing you need to do before you move into an exercise campaign of any kind is to have a conversation with your physician. What can I do, what am I capable of, what do I need to avoid given the risk factors that I have and the medications that I'm on. You can't provide some kind of a generic summary for everyone. It has to be unique. But the bottom line is exercise works. It works for everyone in every age and the effects are instantaneous.

There are a lot of people selling pills, potions, and hormones out there with all kinds of claims about what they can do. Guess what? All the benefits that are associated with any of the pills and potions including nutritional supplements, you can get for free with exercise. So, there's no question that it works, and it's an extraordinarily powerful influence in health and quality of life.

NOT EXERCISING? READ THIS

With everything going on in Linda's life, she is not exercising, so I introduced Linda to Tami Anastasia, a health and wellness counselor and the owner of Tams Wellness Studio. Tami is also an Alzheimer's Caregiver Support Group Facilitator and a Certified Senior Advisor.

So many of us know the importance of exercise. I've never heard anybody say, "Oh! Exercise. You don't need to exercise." Nobody says that. Everybody knows it's important. Even so, Linda has much going on in her life with her parents, work, and taking care of her family that exercising is difficult. What does someone like Linda do when it becomes too difficult? When you know you're supposed to do it, but you just don't? Why do you think that happens and what suggestions can you give to Linda?

That's a great question because, if you look at it, today most people know the importance of exercise and our culture has made exercise a much more complicated issue than it needs to be. Our culture spends much more time focusing on changing the behavior and not enough attention is given to the thoughts that we have associated with the behavior. One of the main reasons why people have difficulty changing a behavior or habit, just because of psychological barrier called resistance.

Now, that being said, I want to start off by saying this, that there is not something inherently wrong with people who have difficulty making lifestyle changes. In other words, the problem is not that people are lazy or that they lack self-discipline or determination or the will; the problem is in the rules they're trying to follow. Our cultural standards and recommendations that people are trying to meet are often unrealistic for the individual. I say that they're unrealistic because the cultural standards and recommendations do not take into consideration the individual needs of a person, their limitations, their abilities and their interests. What happens is a lot of people bite off more than they can chew and it's just a matter of time before they physically or mentally burn out. The key to making an exercise a habit or changing any lifestyle habit is figuring out what's going to work for you. That's going to vary from person to person. I think we need to give people an understanding, you need to know what resistance is, why resistance occurs and what triggers resistance.

Resistance gets often mislabeled as being lazy, as being difficult, or lacking self-discipline, determination or will. It's none of the above. Resistance is a subconscious defense mechanism that gets triggered to protect us from experience pain, anger, frustration, disappointment, judgment and/ or criticism. It's a subconscious defense mechanism that gets triggered which means, most of the time people aren't even aware that it's been triggered. What triggers resistance is a few different things when we try to force ourselves to do things we're not ready to do or we don't want to do. Resistance can also get triggered when we're tired of being told what we should do and how we should do it, which our culture is famous for doing. We're also going to meet resistance when we feel we're being judged or criticized for the way we do something. Often, the most common thing that I see occurs is when people place demands or expectations on themselves that exceed their limitations, that exceeds what they can do on a long-term basis. We can stick anything on a short-term basis but long-term is a different story.

With the stress she is under, Linda is scared about her own health. How can she get on track?

I think the confusion is around trying to figure out what's going to work with me she I can stick to on a regular basis. I don't care what age the person is. I've had clients as young as ten and as old as 98. It's really figuring out how can I make exercise a part of my life in a way that I can look forward to doing it. Our thoughts basically control what we do and so if there's any negative psychological association with our goals or expectations then it's going to decrease the chances of doing it or maintaining it on a regular basis. Let me give you an example. How many people do you know — and yourself included — who like to do things that are time-consuming, painful, or boring? Those are the three most popular ways that people describe exercise. It's no wonder people have difficulty motivating themselves to exercise if we associate it with being time-consuming, painful, or boring. The key is to put exercise into a frame of mind or any behavior change you want to make so that it's associated with pleasure. It's not associated with pain in any way. I don't think we can say that people are waiting too long and then they have a health scare. I think that people truly have a desire but they don't know how to incorporate a behavior into their life in a way that works for them, in a way that's manageable.

What I do is try to help people set goals that are realistic because the bottom line is consistency has to do with our goals and expectations. The more unrealistic our goals and expectations are, the more inconsistent people are going to be. The more realistic our goals and expectations are, the more consistent people are going to be. Let me give you another example. How many people, including yourself, how many of you look forward to doing things that you enjoy doing and how many of you look forward to doing things you don't want to do? Once a behavior gets associated in any way that is physically or psychologically demanding, resistance is going to occur. There are four warning signs that are going to let you know when resistance is occurring. We blame and we shame ourselves, we feel guilty, we're critical of ourselves. I want people to realize, if they're meeting the wall of resistance, it's for a very good reason. It is not because they're lazy. It's not because they lack determination or the will. They're hitting the wall of resistance because they're asking more from themselves than what is realistic at the time.

Here are the four warning signs:

- *One is people are going to have difficulty motivating themselves and/or maintaining the motivation. In other words, they're probably biting off too much more than they can chew and they're having difficulty maintaining it or they're having difficulty motivating themselves because the demand or the expectation or the behavior change or the goal is exceeding what they can realistically do.*

- *The second warning sign is that people are going to avoid or put off the task or goal and have excuses for not doing it.*

- *The third warning sign that's going to let people know that resistance is occurring is they're going to lose interest in the idea of pursuing the goal or changing the behavior completely. They're frustrated. They've given up and they're done. They've lost interest in the idea.*

- *The fourth most telling sign when resistance is occurring is you're going to do the exact opposite of what you say you're going to do.*

Linda mentioned she had gained some weight and wanted to lose a few pounds. She did try exercising and setting some goals, but she's not seeing the results she would like.

That's an excellent point. As a matter of fact, if you ever want to get discouraged about exercise or making any lifestyle changes, the worst thing you can do is to step on a scale. We have been conditioned to think that weight loss is the only benefit of exercise, of changing our eating habits, when in reality, weight loss does not determine the value of what we do. Weight loss can be a benefit down the road but there are so many benefits that occur before we lose a single pound. What I have to teach people is how to measure the benefits in a way that they see a payoff. The payoff happens immediately, it's just that we are not conditioned to see or measure the benefits in a way that we can see that it's paying off.

I have what I call the personal value and benefits of exercise. To give you an idea of the power of this, just for myself, I had 5 clients for 30 days not weigh themselves but I wanted them to keep track that after every time they exercise, I wanted them to write down something that made them feel good, that they could see a payoff. They had more energy. They were on a better mood. They felt stronger. They didn't have to take a nap in the middle of the day. One client said, "I didn't bite my boss' head off at work. I went for a walk around the block instead." I mean, they keep a list of all these valuable, beneficial ways they saw how exercise was paying off.

They kept very motivated and then I had them step on the scale. What do you think happened when they realized they only lost a pound in 30 days? Some of them lost no weight and some of them gained weight. What do you think happened when all the stuff that they wrote down and how they felt about all this positive benefits? What do you think happened the minute they stepped on the scale and they did not see "weight loss"? They got discouraged.

There's a cause and effect relationship and so if I'm going to make behavior changes. If I'm going to change my exercise and I'm going to try walking a mile a day or I'm going to walk once every other day, whatever that is, you have to make a commitment to see how it's paying off because there's a benefit every single time you move. If we are only dependent on measuring the benefit in terms of weight loss, we're going to get discouraged. I can take a person who's a plus size and I can have that person, I can improve their quality of life and their quality of life can improve whether they gain or lose a single pound. I can have them increase and improve their quality of life whether or not they lose a single pound. That's really what the work is about. It's about how to improve people's quality of life and measuring the benefits in a way that are positive instead of measuring them in a way that are discouraging.

I wanted to know about the psychological aspects of making exercise a habit. I asked Tami to talk to us more about that.

What I've learned is, a lot of the psychological roadblocks or the barriers that get in our way with exercise will also carry over into other aspects of our lives so if we can break the habit and break these barriers, break through these barriers they also will help make a difference in other areas of our lives.

I've identified what I call six faulty exercise mindset traps people fall into. I described in the book what they are. I have a lot of self-assessment questionnaires. I provide a lot of personal and professional anecdotes. I provide a lot of different tips and strategies on how to break through the barriers. That is a very concrete, something substantial that they can put into practice at any time of the day, any time of the month, any time of the year whenever they're ready. It really normalizes the frustrations because what the book does, it doesn't shame people, it doesn't blame people. As a matter of fact, I replace what I call the no pain no gain philosophy with the no pain no blame approach. In other words, I meet people where they're at. I'm not going to tell you what you should be doing and how you should be doing it. That's what our culture's doing that's stripping people up.

I'm giving you permission and the skills to figure out how to incorporate lifestyle habits, exercise especially in a way that works for you because the bottom line is, when we do what works for us, we're most likely going to stick to it. If we try doing more than what is realistic for us, the chances are it's going to be short-term and we're going to constantly be in consistent with our habits. I truly believe most people know what is best for them, we've just gotten sidetracked because we're trying to live up to our cultural standards and recommendations that are unrealistic.

I just want to help people to find what it is that's going to be best for them, not based on my expectations but what they're capable of doing. There's so much confusion, there's so much frustration right now because we keep getting this mixed messages and we got to get back to basics. The basics is I want you to move your body in a way that makes you feel good. I want you to choose activities or exercises in a way that you enjoy, choose what you enjoy. When I start working with any people, I always go through, a lot of people go through a medical history, well I go through an exercise history. Tell me about your relationship with exercise, the pluses and the minuses. What works? What hasn't work? What you like? What you don't like? We work off of that.

I can have a client who weighs 350 pounds and if I can get her walk up and down her hallway and it's for a minute or 2, we're doing great because I'm taking her from nothing.

What you don't know is if we do it just right, that 2 or 3 minutes eventually will become 5 minutes, as she gets in more conditioned. Then that 5 minutes may become 10 minutes and 10 minutes may become 15 and it might take us 3 months, 6 months or 10 months or a year to get there but if she pushes or he pushes himself just right each time, how is it that's working against you? What's working against us is trying to do too much too soon and burning out physically and mentally. I have to say, less is a better on a consistent basis than trying to do more and then ultimately doing nothing at all.

I asked Tami what she thought Linda's next steps should be:

The first thing I would really like Linda to start thinking about is instead of wasting her time and energy being judgmental and critical of herself, I want her to look at if she's not doing something, I want her to be very compassionate and understand that the resistance is occurring for a reason. What I want her to do is I want her to modify that goal and I want her to simplify it. I want her to see if she can achieve, do something very, very small and be able to meet it every four weeks because if she can meet that goal every four weeks, then she's most likely doing something that's realistic. Instead of being critical and judgmental, be compassionate and understanding.

Instead of beating your head against the wall and keep trying to force yourself to do the same thing over and over again, simplify it. Reduce your expectations. Change them. Modify them and set yourself up to be successful instead of setting yourself up to fail. Be very gentle and patient with yourself because every single person out there has the ability but you just got to find what works for you, not what our culture says, not what your husband says or your best friend. It's figuring out what works for you and stick to that because then that is the right thing for you to do.

I talked with Linda enough to know that she is going to take Tami's suggestions seriously and begin an exercise program that appeals to her.

PROVEN TECHNIQUES FOR A BETTER LIFE

Not only is exercise important, but also just being in tune with particular breathing techniques can help reduce stress and live a more productive life. I introduced Linda to Jude Bijou, a respected psychotherapist, professional educator, workshop leader, and long-time student of Eastern philosophy. Her theory of *Attitude Reconstruction*, which is also the title a book she wrote, evolved over the course of more than 30 years of working with clients as a licensed marriage and family therapist.

The hands-on process that grew out of this life-long learning, presented in her book, integrates the worlds of Western psychology, Eastern philosophy, and body-based techniques for accessing and expressing emotions in order to create lasting behavioral change.

I asked her to tell Linda about the book and what the catalyst was that made Jude want to write it.

I grew up not being happy, and figured that there had to be a manual somewhere that I was just missing. As I looked around, I didn't find anything in Western thought, through school, went over to the East and started to pick up pieces there. Then I became a psychotherapist, and all of those elements had to come together, my drive to say, "Okay, I want to feel happier, and I want to help people." It all came together in the realm of emotions, and really understanding the importance of expressing our emotions constructively.

From there, it grew out into, "Gee, what are the kind of thoughts that are going to be helpful?" "How do we communicate in ways that are helpful?" "How do we take action?" Everything really grew out of that initial desire to find personal happiness.

The book has not only helped many people, but it helped me as well. It had to be spiritual, but also extremely practical. My father was a behavioral child psychologist, and so

I had to be concrete. I thought of how the pieces are going to come together, and how we can apply them really practically. That is what it is, because it's not a book that you have to read cover to cover. It's like, "Oh, I'm interested in communication," read that. "Oh, I'm interested in changing my thinking, or dealing with my emotions." It had to be very practical, but also resonate within as being correct, as feeling, "Oh, I can do this."

With all the issues Linda has to deal with, including her own children, her parents, and being part of the Sandwich Generation — and moving through her life at such a fast pace, how can she deal effectively with her emotions?

I think that what we got is really bad messages from our parents, and from our society, growing up, that says, "Don't handle them. Pretend that everything's okay." As children, it was all right to have a temper tantrum, or to cry, or to be afraid, but as we grew up, we got those messages that say, "Don't do it, don't do it." What we then did is internalize that sadness, and that anger, and that fear. That's what I really discovered — when we have those emotions bottled up, they start to come out in very predictable ways that aren't very pleasant, don't connect us with other people, and don't connect us with ourselves. I discovered that all of our problems stem back to unexpressed sadness, anger and fear.

We start out by getting that emotions are really physical, pure sensations in the body. Emotion, energy in motion, that's what the word means. There are not a lot of words, we overlay it with words, but it's a pure sensation in the body. When we feel the emotion of anger, our body heats up, and we want to strike out. That's very different from the energy when we're afraid or anxious, whereas we're colder and feel agitated. Or, when we feel sadness, we feel down and we feel a heaviness. They're just sensations in the body.

If we give ourselves permission to emote, to handle those emotions physically but constructively, and naturally, then the energy moves out of our body and doesn't get stuck. Instead of being overwhelmed, and freaking out, and anxious, and nervous, we can shake and shiver, like a dog at the vet, or a leaf on a tree, and just, "Whoo!" I'm shaking my arms, and my legs, and I'm moving that energy out, because what we do is, instead of doing what the body wants to do, which is to move that agitation energy, we tighten up. Instead of tightening up, we shake it out.

It seems so silly, and so ridiculous, but it works, to just let that energy out, to just shake it, and I'm making sounds, that's the constructive. I'm not going, "Oh, my gosh, I've got so much to do, I've got so much to do!" I'm going, "Whoo! I just have to move this energy out of my body. Whoo!" I'm owning it as mine, and just releasing it.

Linda said to Jude, "You know, I don't sleep much. I've got a child going into college, and we have to pay for that. I've got a parent diagnosed with Alzheimer's, and they didn't plan well, so we're having to help pay for that. Any suggestions?"

I would deal with this on the emotional level, because that's a lot of fear, a lot of what-ifs, what's going to happen in the future, and trying to juggle so many things. I do need to shake and shiver, to move that energy out, because otherwise, my head is just going to keep spinning, and I'll just be in the same old ruts. I'm going to shake out that energy.

While I'm doing it, or after I'm doing it, I'm going to use my thinking, to support myself to calm down. We want to feel more peace; the opposite of fear is peace. Rather than feeling agitated, we want to feel calm, and then act and take care of all of those things from a calm place. We can say to ourselves, "Everything will be all right. Everything is all right. I'll handle one thing at a time. One thing at a time. Everything is going to be all right."

Do that kind of self-talk, where we're interrupting the old thinking, the freaking ourselves out thinking, and bringing in the reality. "All right. I'll handle it, one at a time. One thing at a time. One thing at a time." Just by doing that with the mind, we can calm the body, and then we can deal with what needs to be addressed at that particular time.

I asked Jude to talk about the title of her book, *Attitude Reconstruction*, and her perspective about how attitude affects our lives.

Attitude, really, is all encompassing. There are just basic ways that we think, and ways that we communicate, and ways that we act. It's an attitude that we take on. What I realized was that, with sadness, when we don't deal with the sadness, we take those attitudes on about ourselves. We feel negative about ourselves. I feel unworthy, and I feel co-dependent, or dependent on other people, or I feel passive, and I'm hard on myself.

Those are core attitudes that we all have, some more than others, but they indicate that I just need to start to allow myself to cry some more, and start telling myself those positive messages, interrupting the old messages. That's the kind of bad thinking, and bad attitudes that we take on about ourselves, that have to do with unexpressed sadness.

Unexpressed anger is what we take out on other people. "You should be different. I have an expectation, and you're not living up to it." Those are the kinds of things, I'm out there, my focus is on, that "you're not okay, and you should do it my way." That kind of thinking, those are the bad attitudes, the core bad attitudes, that really indicate that the person has a lot of unexpressed anger.

It's so important to get, nobody else is angry at that person. This is my anger. Rather than focusing on, "If they would only be like this, and they didn't do this." All that kind of stuff is only going to make you feel worse, and you feel angrier and more separate. We have to own it, about, "Gosh, my parents did the best they could. That's over." People are they way they are, not the way I want them to be.

We need to coach ourselves, and put in the reality that now is the time. "All right, I've got to let some of that stuff go, so that I can be the person that I want to be. I can be that person that is full of joy and love and peace, because that's who I want to be. I don't want to be holding on to all of those other things."

It's so important to accept other people for their differences, because then we can do what we need to do to take care of ourselves, but from a loving place, not from an angry place.

Linda feels that she has so much to do, and she is just overwhelmed. Jude had good advice for her.

Overwhelm means that we need to take a look and see what kinds of messages we keep telling ourselves. Whether we keep freaking ourselves out with, "Oh, I've got so much to do," or whether we're going around and judging everybody negatively, with those shoulds, and "They should be different." Or whether we're putting ourselves down, and going, "Oh, that was stupid. Oh, you made another mistake. Oh, gosh, nobody likes you."

We can start to identify those kinds of thoughts that don't serve us well, that we picked up really early, when we couldn't deal with our emotions, when we no longer had permission to express them physically and let them out of our body. We can start to interrupt those, and then slap in what contradicts it, what's true.

It's true that, "One thing at a time. I'll handle the future in the future." So much more pacifying than thinking, "Oh my gosh! Oh..." We can systematically replace those old thoughts with what is true.

An affirmation is something that we wish was true. "I have all of the abundance that I need," but maybe you don't. Maybe you have bills to pay, and you're in a financial crunch. Repeating what's not true isn't going to help as much as being really focused on the reality. "All right, I need to get a job, or I need to get a second job. Okay." Don't freak out about the future too much, stay with what's going to help you right now.

Linda does have a very difficult situation, a situation that she's kind of stuck with. She told me she asks herself, "How did this happen to me? I've got my parent who has Alzheimer's and occasionally forgets who I am." Jude responded to suggest to Linda how to handle this type of situation:

It's very stressful, absolutely. I'd say, again, take care of yourself first, because then you have the energy, and can be positive about offering service to other people, rather than going with that, "Oh, I don't want to do it, and how come I got here?" That's not really helpful, rather than, "I have to accept the lot that I have been given in life," Then I can turn within, and say, "Well, now what do I do with that? What is the best thing to do with my parents?" Or, "What do I need to do? Do I need to look for a new job?"

We can ask within, especially if we start to handle our emotions, and start to watch our thinking, and keep our thinking to support ourselves in a positive way. We can start to hear what that quiet voice is. Not that chatter in our mind, that goes, "Oh, you should do this, and why did this happen, and so on." We can really start to focus on what we know within ourselves, because that's where truth really resides.

Then we go, "Okay, I have to accept that my parents are in declining health, and what do I need to do? What do I need to do? What's called for here?" Then we can line up with that, rather than resisting. We need to get clear, by turning within, and asking ourselves, and then listening to the answer.

I interjected, "Jude, you include 33 destructive attitudes in the book. Can you take one of them, let's say the one of being overwhelmed, or being excessively worried, and briefly go through the attitude reconstruction process?"

Absolutely, and that's just the one that came to my mind was worry. When we can't sleep at night, that's worry. The emotion there is fear, and so I really recommend that, even though it just sounds really ridiculous, is to shake that energy out of the body. Do it for like a minute or two, and it feels so good, and it relaxes the body, and the thinking just all calms down.

Then you can think, "All right. Okay. I feel better. Now, I can do that re-wiring, I've attended to the emotion." Or, maybe, if I'm angry, I've had that little hissy fit, or had that cry. Then I can attend to my thoughts. "All right, how can I line up my thoughts to support me to do what I need to do? I've got so much that I'm worried about, let me write them all down." Then I can look, again, turn within and look, "All right, which of these really are important? What needs my attention first?"

Then, as we go and make a list of what we need to, we can be nice and specific, because when we worry, we can just catapult ourselves way into the future and over-generalize. Where, if we can stay nice and focused on one thing at a time, one thing at a time. Then, when we talk, we don't talk in those always and nevers. We can think, "All right, this is what needs attention." Those kinds of things will help with worry, I would keep myself focused on one thing at a time, and that, "I can do it, I can handle it, this will pass."

Linda told me that Jude's suggestions were great because they don't take much time and something she can work on anytime. She's going to start using Jude's suggestions right away.

REDUCING OUR RISK OF DEMENTIA

Because of Linda's mother being diagnosed with dementia and her father showing signs of cognitive impairment, she is concerned about herself. She had asked me if there are things she can do to prevent — or at least reduce — her chances of getting dementia.

To help address her concerns, I introduced Linda to Patricia Spilman, a neuroscientist with over 20 years of experience in neurodegenerative disease research, including twelve years with world-renowned neuropathologist, Stephen J. DeArmond, and a Nobel Laureate, Stanley Prusiner, at the University of California, San Francisco.

For the last ten years, Patricia's focus has been on the development of new therapeutics as part of an Alzheimer's Disease drug discovery team following a pharmaceutical industry model in an academic research setting in the Bredesen Lab. This work resulted in one candidate entering clinical trials. The lab, the John Bredesen Drug Discovery Lab, continues this work that started at the Buck Institute for Research on Aging in

Novato, California, and at the Mary S. Easton Center for Alzheimer's Disease Research at UCLA.

Alzheimer's is such an important subject, and I asked Patricia to talk more about her research and what made her get into this particular field.

When I was in college, I had a very good friend and I was at his family table, and the woman of the family burst out in tears and said, "My husband is sitting next to me, but the man that I love is gone." We were all so startled. He had just gotten a diagnosis of Alzheimer's disease. I had just learned about it. It was such a surprise to me as a young person to find out that your body can remain relatively healthy while your cognitive abilities — your ability to remember or think — can decline due to a disease. It was so moving and so dramatic that I knew it was the field that I wanted to go into to understand better and, of course, now recently, to help find a cure for.

I read an article on something Patricia had said that led into our discussion: "While I have devoted my career to the discovery of an effective treatment for Alzheimer's disease, I would rather people never experience cognitive decline and never need treatment for Alzheimer's. To that end, I have assembled a comprehensive overview of the known risk factors for Alzheimer's disease based on epidemiological studies and scientific experimentation and what to do to address them. Not all Alzheimer's disease is avoidable, as some disease has a strong genetic basis, but I hope, by sharing this information, more people will be able to prevent or at least delay the onset of cognitive decline." I thought that that was very profound and asked her to talk about Alzheimer's in terms of a cure. Are we close?

We're not close. The word "cure" is the word of the great optimist. I like to think that I am one because I do dedicate so much time to this. It's probably more realistic to say that through a combination of lifestyle, diet changes and maybe some drug therapy, we can preserve cognitive function for longer or delay the onset of decline. Certainly, there are a lot of health issues with aging persons. A cure is a bit unlikely, although it's certainly something we're always shooting for as well as earlier and better diagnosis, which would certainly help address the issue of cognitive decline.

WHAT ABOUT PREVENTION?

I absolutely believe that if an older person really does increase their exercise, has a good diet, participates in life, and keeps challenging themselves intellectually, it indeed lowers the risk for Alzheimer's Disease. It will never be zero, but certainly there are people out there of a very advanced age who do not suffer from cognitive decline. I do believe that we can really make some headway if we get the information out there, which, of course, you're helping to do.

After Linda and I discussed exercise with other experts in the field, we wanted to ask Patricia about hearing things like, "Go for walks three days a week" and "Don't just do aerobic exercise, because you've got build muscles, as well." What should we believe?

Believe all of it. Just get out there. Get moving. Start exercising. I know scientists really want to quantify things. Often, people want to hear, "Oh, I want to exercise 30 minutes a day, three days a week. That's the dose I'm going to take." In reality, exercise is an everyday thing. It involves a variety. Sometimes it's walking. Sometimes it's dancing around, playing golf, playing tennis. Embrace all of it. Do all of it. Don't set out a certain amount that you're going to do.

I will say though that strength building is an important component of it because strength building, keeping your muscle mass up is really, really good for your brain. It induces production of something called Brain-derived Neurotropic Factor, which is sort of a mouthful, but, essentially, just means it's a factor in the brain that's really good for the cells of the brain, the neurons. Weight training really helps with that.

Combine movement, aerobics, walking and strength training in a variety of ways that's fun and enjoyable for you, combined with social activity. Golf can be social, so can walking with a friend. It's really one of the best ways to exercise and keep the brain healthy.

I had suggested to Linda that she take time to listen to music more often, and maybe even learn an instrument, but she feels she doesn't have time for that. Patricia offered some motivation to give Linda a new perspective about music.

I'm so glad you mentioned music. It's so, so important for brain health. People who play a musical instrument or sing in groups or really enjoy music stimulate areas of the brain that are important for neurogenesis, and that means the formation of new brain cells and, as the name would suggest, new neurons.

I recently read that music stimulates more areas of the brain than even language. Musical memory is one of the last to go. I just saw a beautiful documentary, Alive Inside, about memory and music that showed that when people — even those with advanced dementia — get to enjoy the music of their youth again, it lights them up. It literally lights them up, and they remember not just the music, but they start talking about other memories, friends they used to have, things they used to do. It is an absolute tonic, that really does help cognition.

You mentioned learning an instrument. Oh, it's so true. In fact, I give talks where I use PowerPoint slides, and on one slide I have a harmonica and bongos, because most people will balk a little at a very complicated instrument like a violin, but Linda can pick up a harmonica and learn how to play, get a book and learn how to play. Of course, bongos, there's so much joy in playing drums and percussion. I guess you could argue there's some exercise involved as well.

The one instrument we always have with us is our voice. Sing out in the shower, in the car, and, hopefully, around other people. That, too, is really good for your brain.

I asked Patricia about other areas she thinks people should emphasize to hopefully reduce their chance of cognitive decline.

Right now, my interest is on how we output ourselves into the world and how that can help our mind. Enjoying laughter, humor, and comedy is for short-term memory and for brain health and for releasing stress. Stress, of course, it's great to say, "Well, I have a low-stress life," but most of us can't control the stresses in our life. What we can do is respond to stress with stress-relieving activities. Certainly, yoga and meditation are found to really help with stress on a scientific level. There're a lot of peer-reviewed publications on that.

I like finding in that same literature the effects of laughter. It raises one's pain threshold. Of course, pain can be quite a stressor for older people. It made me recall a book from many years ago written by Norman Cousins called Anatomy of an Illness where he treated his own rare form of arthritis by prescribing himself comedies, and I think he particularly liked the Marx Brothers, and how much it helped him heal. It's a very real phenomenon.

I think this would be clear as well, continued intellectual stimulation. I think I'll say, unfortunately, for a lot of people, they sort of picture a life arc where they learn a lot in their youth, they employ it a lot in early adulthood, in middle age and career, but they have might not pursue it as much as they get older, which is a wrong way to look at the world. It should be a time after career to really start learning new things, read more, take classes, learn something and teach it. The brain just loves that. You have to convince your brain that you're still 25 if you want it to perform like you're 25.

Sleep is always needed. We absolutely have to have quality sleep to have memory consolidation and the ability to keep learning and functioning. It's so critical. I'm glad that you brought it up. Sleep issues have to be addressed.

Dr. Bredesen sees some individuals with cognitive decline. I asked him, "What are the top things that you see again and again that, in your opinion, lead to what we call mild cognitive impairment?" Of course, he did say stress and he said, "Poor quality sleep." There, of course, are sleep centers that people can go to and ways that they can help themselves sleep better, but it's absolutely critical. Exercise improves sleep.

Linda's takeaway from Patricia included a new view of the benefits of laughing, socializing, learning new skills, moving her bodies, eating whole foods, getting enough sleep, and relieving stress through healthy outlets — basically, living life to the fullest.

GENETICS AND PROGRESSION

Linda wanted to know if having a parent who's been diagnosed with some form of dementia like Alzheimer's meant she has a little more to worry about. This is what Patricia told her:

It's a very good question. It's a complicated one. I think that you might really appreciate some science on this. There are types of Alzheimer's Diseases that are called familial. They involve genetic mutations that lead to what we call Early Onset Alzheimer's disease. That typically means the Alzheimer's Disease that manifests before the age of 60. In general, if it's Alzheimer's disease that appears after, say, age 60, 65, 70, then that's late onset. Really, for most people, it's in the 70s or 80s.

If there is a genetic component to that, it's actually the expression of what we just call a genetic variant called apolipoprotein 4. I had to throw out one large word there, but that protein in the brain helps with lipid metabolism in the inflammatory response. It has a lot of different roles in the brain. People can have one of three kinds. There is an apolipoprotein 1, but it's almost unheard of. There are 2, 3, and 4. We get a copy from both of our parents, so we have two copies of this. People who have two copies of apolipoprotein 4 are at higher risk for Alzheimer's disease.

Even if you have that component and your parent did, you can still lower your risk by the same methods that anybody does. Perhaps, it becomes even more important to you then to exercise, to keep your intellectual pursuits up, to relieve your stress, to have good nutrition. I think it's even worth getting genetically tested to see if one is APOE-4 so that they know that they have a task ahead of them to keep their brain functioning well.

What about the effects of social interaction for someone who has already been diagnosed and might be at that early to mid-stage level of the disease? Linda said her mother had been very outgoing in the past but now just wants to be alone or maybe sit in front of the TV. In my work as an advisor around these issues, I've heard family members and adult children say, "Well, that's what mom wants. She doesn't want to do anything. And I'm not going to force her." I asked Patricia what she would say to someone in that situation.

That's a really important issue. Post-diagnosis, there are often the symptoms of apathy or what we call "anhedonia," which is not caring so much about the things that we used to care about, whether it's paying bills or taking a walk. I do think it's really good in those cases to discuss this with the family and the friends of the person who's received the diagnosis to find ways to keep the individual, the patient or client involved in life. Sometimes, it involves changing how one interacts with them.

I'll give you an example because my father-in-law does suffer from Alzheimer's Disease. This did make some people pull away from him because his behavior changed. We spent some time understanding what he can do now and the timeframe in which he can answer questions, and we do it his way. Everything is right in the moment. One has to be very patient. You can see him really start to engage and light up again. Even if you're willing to point to the same picture in the newspaper a few times, you can change what you say about it, they keep interacting because he doesn't have short-term memory, or even walking through a garden, "Oh, there is a rose. There is a pansy," right there in the moment.

Don't ask questions that challenge memory over and over again because that's what can be quite a stressor for people with memory decline. Unwittingly, their loved ones will say, "Well, don't you remember that?" or, "Do you remember Joe?" It's a way of talking that we use all the time. It has to be rewired so that the person with the diagnosis doesn't pull back and feel awkward as well.

I suggested to Linda that she and her siblings should attend seminars or workshops to learn how to better communicate with their parents, considering the dementia and cognitive decline. I know from my experience with the issue that if what Linda is looking for is a discussion with their parents, instead of talking about what they did this morning or yesterday, she's likely to make more of a connection talking about what they did many years ago. Patricia chimed in:

Oh, that can often work really well because the way Alzheimer's typically progresses is the short-term memory goes first, and then recent memories maybe going back a year, but, indeed, very old memories are preserved really until the end, especially sense memories, musical memories, memories that have to do with smell. It can be very enjoyable to engage the friend, loved one, client, patient in discussions of their old memories especially combined with stimulation that helps them to remember something like music from that time period, or even a smell or other sensory experience.

Patricia ended by sharing with Linda some sites she could go to learn more about what Patricia and her colleagues are doing, so Linda could continue to stay informed on these issues.

Of course, I have great admiration for the Alzheimer's Association. They have an excellent website: http://www. alz.org/. They keep up with and present the latest in research on Alzheimer's disease.

The Buck Institute for Research on Aging in Novato, California, also has a really great website http://www. thebuck.org/. You can go and look at what the Bredesen Lab is doing there and Dr. Bredesen's work with patients.

The Mary S. Easton Center for Alzheimer's Disease Research at UCLA puts out a newsletter, and it presents our research as well as that of others at UCLA. Just go to the Easton Center website at,http://www.eastonad.ucla. edu/ and ask for an electronic copy of the newsletter.

Linda does feel better about the hereditary issue of the disease and will continue doing various things to lessen the chances of getting dementia — with exercise at the top of the list.

* * *

Though Linda is a wonderful daughter and is always putting her parents before anything else in her life right now, she will not be a help to her parents or the rest of her family if she doesn't take care of herself. She has begun to really see the truth in that, and she's changing her habits to take better care of herself.

CHAPTER EIGHT

Recap for Linda

Linda has a lot on her plate, but she's realizing she has people she can lean on for guidance. Let's take a look back at the chapters and some of the key takeaways for Linda, which she has turned into the list below of meaningful actions she can take.

Just having this list and knowing it's based on advice from experts she trusts has done a lot to reduce her anxiety and give her hope that she can manage the journey of caring for her aging parents — and managing her own experience as she ages, too.

Chapter One — Family Communications

- Coordinate a family meeting or conference call with agenda to determine parents' care needs and assign tasks to all siblings.

- Determine who Power of Attorney(s) will be and contact an Elder Law Attorney to produce needed documents.

- Have family members attend educational sessions through the Alzheimer's Association or other forum.

- Manage parents' finances involving her father in the process and get advice from a financial advisor on affordability of care for parents.

Chapter Two — Paying for Long-Term Care

- Make sure parents have full Medicare Advantage coverage.

- Talk to Elder Care Attorney on setting up parent's irrevocable trust in order to get approved for Medicaid and Veteran's long-term care benefits.

- Check to see if any life insurance policies are still in place. If so, continue to pay premiums or consider selling policies to help pay for care.

- Look into long-term care insurance for Linda and her husband.

Chapter Three — Getting Professional Advice

- Seek geriatric consulting advice to provide assistance in navigating through this entire process.

- Seek advice from a full-service senior placement advisor to know what the options would be should her parents move into senior living while receiving the proper care and supervision.

Chapter Four — The Realities of Long-term Care

- Review in-home care options and costs.

- Compare best in-home care option to assisted living.

- Review local, adult day care options for parents.

- Educate family members on hospice should that become a reality.

Chapter Five — Enhance Seniors Lives Through Technology

- Review technology options available to keep parents safe, including sensors and monitoring for home.

- Upon reviewing in-home care options, look at the technology options they provide while caring for parents.

- Upon reviewing other senior living options, look at the technology options they provide while caring for parents.

Chapter Six — Protecting Your Parents from Abuse

- Educate parents on various senior scams to help decrease their vulnerability and the possibility that they will be taken advantage of.

- Talk to an elder law attorney and/or financial planner about any unusual activities taking place with parents' finances, even if it has to do with family members.

Chapter Seven — Taking Care of YOU

- Exercise.

- Don't keep things inside.

- Exercise

- Breath

- Exercise

- Learn something new (i.e. — instrument)

- Exercise

CHAPTER NINE

Don't Do It Alone

If there is anything that I hope you and Linda gain from this book, it is knowing that there are many resources out there to assist you in your efforts to keep your parents or other loved ones safe. Whether it is home care, assisted living, memory care, legal, insurance, or just general advice to help point you in the right direction, the people and the information are out there! Trying to handle all of this yourself, as a caregiver will not do anybody good. As a matter of fact, you could make the situation worse by causing more stress on yourself and others. A list of resources of many who contributed to this book is provided in Chapter 10.

Statistics show that you are one of more than 65 million adults in North America taking care for older parents, grandparents, spouses, and other older adults.

According to AARP, family caregivers average 20 hours of unpaid in-home care per week and 87 percent of them are not getting enough sleep. Though this may sound like you or someone you know, it could lead to caregiver burnout. Psychologists define it as "a debilitating psychological condition brought about by unrelieved stress." The study shows when caregivers suspect signs of burnout, they're already suffering from numerous conditions.

Of course, this can be related to the loved one's illness but also with financial pressures, disagreements among family members and myriad other issues going on with the family. All in all, this is a formula for caregiver burnout that would have a negative effect for providing proper care for a family member or other loved one. This stress and burning the candle at both ends can be detrimental to a caregiver's own health.

Several organizations, including the National Alliance of Caregiving and Alzheimer's Association, show that most caregivers are ill-prepared for their role and provide care with little or no support, yet more than one-third of caregivers continue to provide intense care to others while suffering from poor health themselves.

It's estimated that women make up about 65% of all caregivers and in today's world more women work outside of the house than ever before. Research shows that female caregivers fare worse than their male counterparts, reporting higher levels of depressive and anxiety symptoms and lower levels of subjective well being, life satisfaction, and physical health than male caregivers.

We have all heard this announcement on an airplane..."In the event of a decompression, an oxygen mask will automatically appear in front of you. To start the flow of oxygen, pull the mask towards you. Place it firmly over your nose and mouth. If you are traveling with a child or someone who requires assistance, secure your mask on first, and then assist the other person." Only when we first help ourselves can we effectively help others. Caring for yourself is one of the most important, and one of the most often forgotten things you can do as a caregiver. When your needs are taken care of, the person you care for will benefit, too. Caregivers are often so concerned with caring for their relative's needs that they lose sight of their own well being.

Remember, you don't have to do this alone! In my day-to-day work, I personally witness caregiver stress as a common phenomenon. By getting advice from experts in the field and taking care of yourself can help to manage stress and improve your physical and mental health to benefit yourself, your parents and others who depend on you.

Resources

Many experts shared their knowledge for this book. You can find out more about the experts and their organizations here:

- S. Jay Olshansky, PhD — University of Illinois-Chicago, www.sjayolshansky.com

- Seth Sternberg — Honor, www.joinhonor.com

- Marcy Baskin, CSA — Senior Care Authority, www.seniorcareauthority.com

- Steve Sisgold — Whole Body Intelligence, www.WholeBodyIntelligence.com

- Jude Bijou, MA, MFT — Attitude Reconstruction, www.AttitudeReconstruction.com

- Sherri Snelling — Caregiving Club, www.caregivingclub.com

- Mary Hulme, LCSW — Moonstone Geriatrics, www.moonstonegeriatric.com

- Pamela C Spahr — Inspired Caregivers, www.inspiredcaregivers.com

- Robert Nations — Senior Helpers North Bay, www.Seniorhelpers.com

- Sanford I. Horowitz — Law office of Sanford I. Horowitz, www.Horowitzelderlaw.com

- Joy Loverde — The Complete Eldercare Planner, www.elderindustry.com

- Shirley Krohn — California Senior Legislature, www.4csl.org

- Christina Irving, LCSW — Family Caregiver Alliance, www.caregiver.org

- Brian May — Summit Life Equity, www.summitlifeequity.com

- Tina Cheplick, RN — Care Solutions for Elders, www.caresolutionsforelders.com

- Tami Anastasia, MA, CSA — TAMS Wellness Studio, www.tamswellness.com

- Carol Marak — Seniorcare.com, www.SeniorCare.com

- Laurie White, MSW — Dementia Consulting, www.dementiaconsulting.com

- Carolyn Rosenblatt — Aging Parents, www.agingparents.com

- Dr. Mikol Davis — Aging Parents, www.agingparents.com

- Jamie Watson, Partner — Gaw Van Male, www.gawvanmale.com

- Christopher Westfall — Freedom Retirement Planning, www.medicareagenttraining.com

- Leslie Whiting — Long-term care Options, www.lesliewhiting.com

- Paula Scoglio — Paliative Care/Hospice RN, www.vitas.com

- Art Maines — Senior Scam Action Associates, www.seniorscamteam.wordpress.com

- Philip P. Lindsley, CELA — San Diego Elder Law Center, www.sandiegoelderlaw.com

- Amy Andonian — Avenidas, www.avenidas.org

- Erik C. Aho, JD, CFE — Aho and Associates, www.ahoandassociates.com

- Victoria L. Collier, CELA — Victoria L. Collier, PC, www.elderlawgeorgia.com

Acknowledgments

In memory of my parents, Ruby and Pauline Samson, my brother Fred Samson and my mother-in-law Gayle Levine.

Thank you to...

All the Lindas out there, who are the caregivers providing the physical and emotional care for a parent, spouse, sibling, or other loved one.

My clients whom I have assisted during their transition of a loved one, who have inspired me to share the knowledge I have gained from each of them with others going through a similar process.

All the hard-working individuals in the health care and senior services industry, especially the Senior Care Authority staff and franchisees throughout the country.

My wife Michèle, my daughter, Brooke, my son Anthony, my son-in-law Jason, my daughter-in-law Kelly, my amazing grandchildren, my brothers — Elliott, and Norm, my sisters in law (who are like my sisters) — Sandra, Marge and Barbara.

My editor, Grace Kerina, who has the patience of a saint.

About the Author

Frank M. Samson is the founder of Senior Care Authority and The Aging Boomers Radio SHOW and Podcast. Before founding his own business which he has franchised nationally, he worked in the franchise and travel industries for over three decades.

Frank's passion for senior care comes from personally experiencing the challenges that face families today. After several years of researching the health care and senior services industries, he began Senior Care Authority to provide elder care consulting and senior placement. Senior Care Authority (www.SeniorCareAuthority.com) began by servicing and assisting families initially in Northern California. The company has franchised its program and now assists families around the country through its network of local, professional Senior Care Authority placement agencies.

His expertise in senior care has given Frank the opportunity to write a regular blog and host a radio show podcast called The Aging Boomers (www.AgingBoomers.com), which also appears on iTunes, iHeart Radio, Spreaker, Stitcher, local radio stations, and is available as a free app on iPhone and Android phones.

Frank is a Certified Senior Advisor (CSA) and is a member of the Section on Aging Chapters and Senior Roundtable groups in Northern California. He is a Certified Senior Advisor, a member of the Society of Certified Senior Advisors, and an Honorary Faculty Member at Michigan State University.

Frank and his family are originally from Michigan, then lived in the Chicago area before moving to Sonoma, California, where he currently lives with his wife Michèle. They are very proud parents and grandparents to their two children and their spouses, and their four grandchildren.

With My Compliments

Thank you for reading this book.

There is not enough space in this short work to include every situation of families planning and caring for their loved ones, though my hope is that the guidance that the experts and I provided to Linda will help you with your particular situation. However, each senior is different and each family's needs are different.

If you would like to email me for advice on your particular needs, please feel free to contact me at frank@ SeniorCareAuthority.com.

As a gift to you, I'm offering a complementary 30-minute consultation to assist with your loved ones needs, whether you need general advice or references for help in your area. To arrange for this free consultation, go to www.SeniorCareAuthority.com/consultation.

Website: www.SeniorCareAuthority.com
Podcasts: www.TheAgingBoomers.com

In two years we've created over 134 bestselling books in a row, 90% from first-time authors. We do this by selecting the highest quality and highest potential applicants for our future programs.

Our program doesn't just teach you how to write a book—our team of coaches, developmental editors, copy editors, art directors, and marketing experts incubate you from book idea to published bestseller, ensuring that the book you create can actually make a difference in the world. Then we give you the training you need to use your book to make the difference you want to make in the world, or to create a business out of serving your readers. If you have life-or world-changing ideas or services, a servant's heart, and the willingness to do what it REALLY takes to make a difference in the world with your book, go to http://theauthorincubator.com/apply/ to complete an application for the program today.

Clarity Alchemy: When Success Is Your Only Option

by Ann Bolender

Cracking the Code: A Practical Guide to Getting You Hired

by Molly Mapes

Divorce to Divine: Becoming the Fabulous Person You Were Intended to Be

by Cynthia Claire

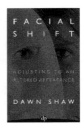

Facial Shift: Adjusting to an Altered Appearance

by Dawn Shaw

Finding Clarity: Design a Business You Love and Simplify Your Marketing

by Amanda H. Young

Flourish: Have It All Without Losing Yourself

by Dr. Rachel Talton

Marketing To Serve: The Entrepreneur's Guide to Marketing to Your Ideal Client and Making Money with Heart and Authenticity

by Cassie Parks

NEXT: How to Start a Successful Business That's Right for You and Your Family

by Caroline Greene

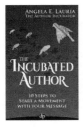

Pain Free: How I Released 43 Years of Chronic Pain

by Dottie DuParcé (Author), John F. Barnes (Foreword)

Secret Bad Girl: A Sexual Trauma Memoir and Resolution Guide

by Rachael Maddox

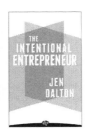

Skinny: The Teen Girl's Guide to Making Choices, Getting the Thin Body You Want, and Having the Confidence You've Always Dreamed Of

by Melissa Nations

The Aging Boomers: Answers to Critical Questions for You, Your Parents and Loved Ones

by Frank M. Samson

The Incubated Author: 10 Steps to Start a Movement with Your Message

by Angela Lauria

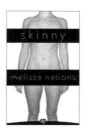

The Intentional Entrepreneur: How to Be a Noisebreaker, Not a Noisemaker

by Jen Dalton (Author), Jeanine Warisse Turner (Foreword)

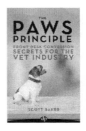

The Paws Principle: Front Desk Conversion Secrets for the Vet Industry

by Scott Baker

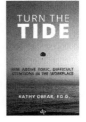

Turn the Tide: Rise Above Toxic, Difficult Situations in the Workplace

by Kathy Obear

Made in the USA
San Bernardino, CA
06 May 2016